for
Professor George John Marcopoulos

an inspired and inspiring teacher

SEMINAR STUDIES   IN HISTORY

The First World War Peace Settlements, 1919–1925

Erik Goldstein

An imprint of **Pearson Education**

London · New York · Toronto · Sydney · Tokyo · Singapore · Hong Kong · Cape Town
New Delhi · Madrid · Paris · Amsterdam · Munich · Milan · Stockholm

PEARSON EDUCATION LIMITE

Head Office:
Edinburgh Gate
Harlow
Essex CM20 2JE
Tel: +44 (0)1279 623623
Fax +44 (0)1279 431059

London Office:
128 Long Acre
London WC2E 9AN
Tel: +44 (0)20 7447 2000
Fax: +44 (0)20 7240 5771
Website: www.history-minds.com

First published in Great Britain in 2002

© Pearson Education, 2002

The right of Erik Goldstein to be identified as author
of this work has been asserted by him in accordance
with the Copyright, Designs and Patents Act 1988.

ISBN 0 582 31145 4

British Library Cataloguing in Publication Data
A CIP catalogue record for this book can be obtained from the British Library

Library of Congress Cataloging in Publication Data
A CIP catalogue record for this book can be obtained from the Library of Congress

10 9 8 7 6 5 4 3 2 1

Typeset by 7 in 10/12 Sabon Roman
Produced by Pearson Education Asia Pte Ltd.
Printed in Malaysia, KVP

The Publishers' policy is to use paper manufactured from sustainable forests.

CONTENTS

INTRODUCTION TO THE SERIES

Such is the pace of historical enquiry in the modern world that there is an ever-widening gap between the specialist article or monograph, incorporating the results of current research, and general surveys, which inevitably become out of date. *Seminar Studies in History* is designed to bridge this gap. The series was founded by Patrick Richardson in 1966 and his aim was to cover major themes in British, European and World history. Between 1980 and 1996 Roger Lockyer continued his work, before handing the editorship over to Clive Emsley and Gordon Martel. Clive Emsley is Professor of History at the Open University, while Gordon Martel is Professor of International History at the University of Northern British Columbia, Canada, and Senior Research Fellow at De Montfort University.

All the books are written by experts in their field who are not only familiar with the latest research but have often contributed to it. They are frequently revised, in order to take account of new information and interpretations. They provide a selection of documents to illustrate major themes and provoke discussion, and also a guide to further reading. The aim of *Seminar Studies in History* is to clarify complex issues without over-simplifying them, and to stimulate readers into deepening their knowledge and understanding of major themes and topics.

ACKNOWLEDGEMENTS

We are grateful to the following for permission to reproduce copyright material:

Map 4 after map in *Atäturk*, published by Longman, reprinted by permission of Pearson Education Ltd (Macfie, A.L. 1994); Map 5 after map in *The Near East Since the First World War*, published by Longman, reprinted by permission of Pearson Education Ltd (Yapp, M. E. 1996).

In some instances we have been unable to trace the owners of copyright material, and we would appreciate any information that would enable us to do so.

CHRONOLOGY

1918

5 January	Lloyd George's Caxton Hall Speech
8 January	President Wilson's Fourteen Points Speech [elaborated on to Congress (11 February); at Mt Vernon (4 July) and NYC (27 September)]
3 March	Treaty of Brest-Litovsk between Russia and Central Powers
4 July	Mehmed VI becomes Ottoman Sultan
6 July	deposed Russian tsar Nicholas II and his family executed
30 September	Armistice with Bulgaria
4 October	German and Austrian governments open negotiations with President Wilson for an armistice
21 October	Czechoslovakia declares independence
30 October	Armistice with Ottoman Empire at Mudros
3 November	Armistice with Austria–Hungary
9 November	Abdication of Wilhelm II as German Emperor and proclamation of a republic
11 November	Armistice with Germany signed at Compiègne
12 November	Abdication of Austro–Hungarian Emperor Karl
13 November	Austria proclaimed a republic
16 November	Hungary proclaimed a republic
24 November	Proclamation of the Kingdom of the Serbs, Croats and Slovenes (Yugoslavia)
14 December	British General Election (the 'Khaki Election')

1919

18 January	Paris Peace Conference opens
21 March	Béla Kun establishes a Communist government in Hungary
7 May	Draft peace treaty presented to Germany
15 May	Greek forces land at Smyrna
16 June	Allies present final version of peace treaty to Germany
21 June	German fleet scuttled at Scapa Flow
22 June	German reichstag agrees to proposed peace treaty, with reservations

28 June	Treaty of Versailles signed with Germany
10 September	Treaty of Saint-Germain signed with Austria
October	1st sitting of ILO
27 November	Treaty of Neuilly signed with Bulgaria

1920

10 January	First meeting of the League of Nations
25 April – 12 October	Russo-Polish War
4 June	Treaty of Trianon signed with Hungary
10 August	Treaty of Sèvres signed with Ottoman Empire
14 August	Czechoslovak-Yugoslav Alliance (precursor of the Little Entente)

1921

19 February	Franco-Polish Alliance
March	Anglo-Soviet Trade Agreement
March	Cairo conference on British Middle East
18 March	Treaty of Riga ends Russo-Polish war
12 November	Opening of the Washington Conference

1922

30 January	1st session of the Permanent Court of International Justice
16 April	German-Soviet Treaty of Rapallo
20 October	Lloyd George resigns as British prime minister
30 October	Mussolini becomes premier of Italy
16 December	1st sitting of PCIJ
26 December	Reparations Commission finds Germany in default

1923

11 January	Occupation of the Ruhr by French and Belgian forces
16 February	Japan returns Kiaochow to China
23 Apr	Czechoslovak-Romanian Alliance
7 Junee	Romanian-Yugoslav Alliance
24 Julyy	Treaty of Lausanne between the Allies and Turkey

1924

| 21 January | Death of Lenin |
| 22 January | 1st MacDonald (Labour) government formed in Britain |

27 January	Italo-Yugoslav Treaty
1 February	Britain extends *de jure* recognition to Soviet government.
9 April	Dawes Plan presented on reorganizing German reparations
16 April	Dawes Plan accepted by Germany
2 October	League unanimously adopts Geneva Protocol
25 October	Publication of the Zinoviev letter in Britain
7 November	2nd Baldwin (Conservative) government formed in Britain

1925

12 March	Britain rejects the Geneva Protocol
5–16 October	Locarno Conference

DIPLOMACY BY CONFERENCE

Date	Place	Issues
1919–20	Paris	Peace treaties with Central Powers
1920 (19–26 April)	San Remo	Territorial problems; assigns Class A mandates; invites Germany to conference at Spa to help set reparations total
1920 (19–22 June)	Hythe and Boulogne	Near East; reparations
1920 (5–16 July)	Spa	Germany submits scheme of reparations payments; Germany signs disarmament engagement; German reparations payments assigned as follows: France 52%, British Empire 22%, Italy 10%, Belgium 8%, smaller powers the rest
1920 (December)	Brussels	Allied-German experts fail to reach agreement of reparations as Allied experts could not agree to accept lower sum than that agreed by political leaders at Boulogne
1921 (24–30 January)	Paris	Allies put forward independent reparations proposals, with German payments spread over 42 years
1921 (21 February–14 March)	London	Allies agree Paris (January) schedule of German payments decided. Germany presents counter-proposals

Date	Place	Issues
1921 (29 April–5 May)	London	Ultimatum to Germany for 1 billion gold Marks of reparations payments by end of month or face occupation of the Ruhr. Germany pays by borrowing in London and accepts schedules
1921–22 (12 November–6 February)	Washington	Naval arms control and East Asian stability
1921 (December)	London	Anglo-French meeting in face of possible German reparations default agree to a Five Power meeting at Cannes
1922 (January)	Cannes	Allies agree to a partial moratorium on German reparations payments in return for greater control of German finances. Also resolved issues on intra-Allied division of reparations receipts
1922 (25 February)	Boulogne	Set agenda for Genoa Conference
1922 (10 April–19 May)	Genoa	Russia; general economic problems (breaks down on French insistence that Russia recognize prewar debt)
1922 (7–14 August)	London	Anglo-French failure to resolve problem of German reparations payments
1922–23 (20 November–4 February)	1st Lausanne	Allied effort to negotiate new peace treaty with Turkey
1922 (9–11 December)	London	War debts
1923 (2–4 January)	Paris	War debts: France rejects British and Italian schemes for bond issues
1923 (23 April–24 July)	2nd Lausanne	Peace treaty with Turkey
1924 (16 July–16 August)	London	Acceptance of the Dawes Plan on German reparations
1925 (5–16 October)	Locarno	Confirmation of frontiers of Franco/Belgian-German borders

Map 1   First World War: Postwar Settlements

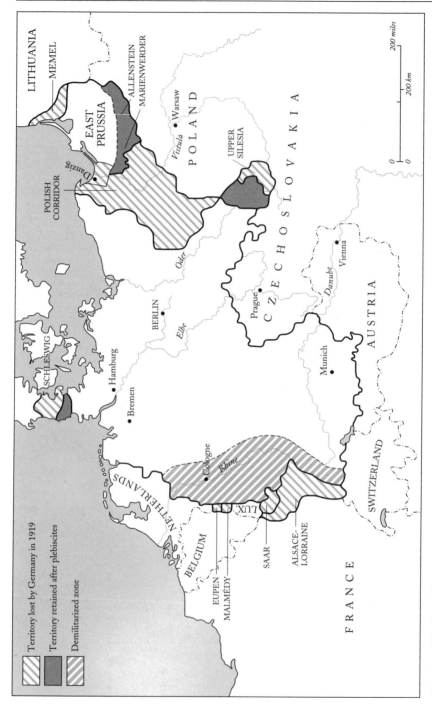

Map 2 The Versailles Settlement, 1919

LITHUANIA

MEMEL

EAST
PRUSSIA

ALLENSTEIN
MARIENWERDER

Warsaw

Vistula

P O L A N D

Danzig

POLISH
CORRIDOR

UPPER
SILESIA

Oder

C Z E C H O S L O V A K I A

Prague

Danube

Vienna

A U S T R I A

SCHLESWIG

BERLIN

Elbe

Hamburg

Bremen

Munich

Cologne

Rhine

SWITZERLAND

NETHERLANDS

LUX.

BELGIUM

EUPEN
MALMÉDY

SAAR

ALSACE-
LORRAINE

F R A N C E

Territory lost by Germany in 1919

Territory retained after plebiscites

Demilitarized zone

200 miles

200 km

0

0

Map 3   The New Europe

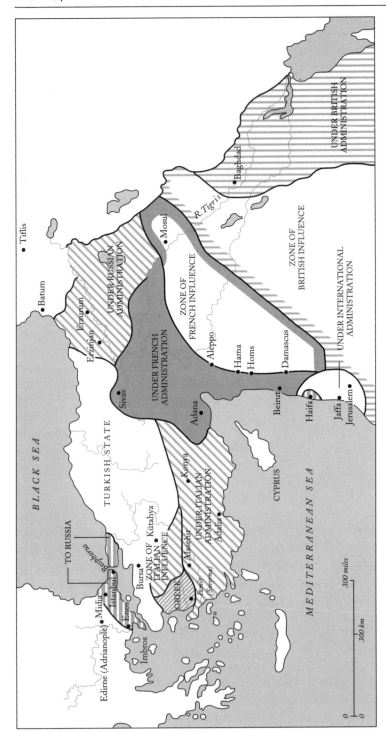

Map 4   The Partition of Turkey

After Macfie, A.L. (1994) *Atatürk*, Longman

Map 5   The Eastern Mediterranean

After Yapp, M.E. (1996) *The Near East Since the First World War*, Longman, p. 253.

Map 6   East Asia

CHAPTER ONE

THE EVE OF THE PARIS PEACE CONFERENCE

In January 1919 leaders, diplomats, soldiers and government officials intent on building a peace settlement after the carnage of the First World War converged upon Paris. One young British diplomat voiced his hope, 'not merely to liquidate the war, but to found a new order in Europe. We were preparing not Peace only, but Eternal Peace.'[1] The Paris Peace Conference would be the largest diplomatic gathering the world had ever known. The victors of the Great War, as the First World War was then called, had come to Paris to shape the postwar order. Although successful in the conflict that had raged for four years, they faced a world of uncertainty. The delegates assembling at Paris could not recall a war such as had just ended in the sheer scale of the devastation and human losses. Between August 1914 and November 1918 sixty million people around the world had been at war, and at the end thirty million lay dead, missing, or wounded. It was a toll that exceeded all previous experience.

The war had finally ended in November 1918 when, in a clearing in the forest near the French city of Compiègne, the German Empire agreed to an armistice. This came into effect at 11 am on 11 November; the eleventh hour of the eleventh day of the eleventh month. The reasons countries had entered the conflict now looked insignificant in comparison to the final impact upon them. France had entered the war with the hope of regaining the provinces of Alsace and Lorraine, lost to Germany in 1871, though by November 1918 France had lost more lives than the entire population of Alsace–Lorraine. The Austro-Hungarian Empire had gone to war hoping to quash the nationalist threat posed by Serbia but by the war's end this empire had collapsed and fragmented into several states. Political turmoil was widespread. The war had seen the fall of many of the dynasties that had dominated Europe for centuries. By November 1918 the monarchs of Germany, Austria–Hungary, and Bulgaria had all fled into exile. Russia had been convulsed by revolution brought on by the turmoil of the war, the Russian tsar deposed and murdered, and the country was now in a state of civil war. Out of this chaos numerous aspiring states had emerged, often with conflicting territorial aspirations and frequently with conflicting would-be governments.

The war had involved twenty-nine countries, in a contest between two opposing camps. The Allies, led by France, Britain, Italy, and Japan, together with Russia until it withdrew from the war after the communist seizure of power in 1917, and joined by the United States in April 1917, fought the Central Powers comprising Germany, Austria–Hungary, Bulgaria, and the Ottoman Empire. As the war ground to its conclusion each of the Central Powers in turn requested an armistice from the Allies, culminating in the German armistice signed at Compiègne. It was intended that these armistices would be followed by a peace conference in which peace treaties would be negotiated between the Allied States and the Central Powers.

Of the myriad problems confronting the peacemakers as they gathered just after the New Year in Paris none was more prominent than the future settlement with Germany. Among the issues to be considered were changes to Germany's frontiers, whether or not it should be forced to pay an indemnity, to what extent its military would be limited in the future, and whether or not there should be trials of those Germans whom the Allies considered to be war criminals. There had already been calls in the British General Election campaign to hang the Kaiser, now in exile in the Netherlands, and the idea of trying the Kaiser found popular favour in all the Allied states. The European allies had promised their electorates that Germany would be forced to pay high financial indemnities, a common practice in many peace settlements. Wilson, however, believed that Germany should only be made liable for damages that were beyond those traditionally allowed by the laws of war. As to Germany's small overseas colonial empire, this was not only eyed avariciously by Britain and France, but Britain's self-governing dominions were also staking their claims.

The Austro-Hungarian Empire had been growing weaker for decades, with mounting tensions between its two dominant ethnic groups, the German-speaking Austrians and the Hungarians, as well as tensions with the many other nationalities of the empire. The diversity of that empire can be seen from the fact that on the eve of the First World War mobilization orders had had to be issued in fifteen languages. Poland, which had ceased to exist as a sovereign state in the eighteenth century when it was divided among Russia, Prussia, and Austria, now re-emerged in the wake of the collapse of those empires; but defining the re-born Poland's frontiers would pose a serious problem.

The war acted as a political cyclone, uprooting and tearing apart this multi-ethnic empire and it was unclear what would emerge out of the wreckage. Ethnic groups previously unrepresented on the international stage were now clamoring for recognition: Czechs, Slovaks, Slovenes, Croats, and Poles. The emergence of these proto-states, however, was only part of the problem of configuring a new political map in central and eastern Europe. Any new frontiers would still leave many minorities within these new states and the problem of how to provide protection for their rights would also have to be considered in any effort to craft a stable new political order.

One of the longest running problems was what had come to be know as the Eastern Question, which concerned the fate of the Ottoman Empire. Since the mid-nineteenth century the Ottoman Empire had been so obviously in decline it was usually referred to as the 'Sick Man of Europe'. With the end of the war Allied forces had entered Constantinople and the Sultan, Mehmed VI, virtually became a prisoner of the Allies. During the war, in a series of secret treaties among themselves, the key European allies had already planned the final carve up of the Ottoman state. By the war's end, however, matters were not so clear. British forces had seized much of the Middle East, including the holy city of Jerusalem, but in the process had made numerous and often conflicting promises as to the postwar settlement. In addition to the series of secret treaties with its main allies it had also supported an Arab revolt, with the implied promise of support for an Arab state, while at the same time promising support for part of the region to be made a national homeland for the Jews. To complicate matters further, President Wilson made it clear that he would have nothing to do with the secret treaties and insisted that the whole matter be resolved using the basic principles outlined in his pronouncements.

Russia was not officially a matter of concern for the peace conference, but the Russian problem permeated the thoughts of the delegates. Russia had fought together with the Allies until 1917 when the communists, led by Lenin, had seized power and withdrawn Russia from the war. This new Russian government was unrecognized by the Allies and, indeed, military support had been provided to anti-communist groups who might bring Russia back into the war in the Allied fold. The allied intervention had been precipitated by the necessities of war, but once the Great War had ended there was dissension among them as to what policy to follow in regard to this new radical regime. Some favoured continued intervention to help topple what they perceived as the wider menace of communist-promoted revolution in other states, while others preferred to move to contain Russia and leave it to its own devices. It was unclear to everyone what the outcome of the internal conflict in Russia would be and, therefore, what role it would play in the postwar world. In order to have some Russian involvement in the peace process a retired Russian foreign minister, Sazonov, was present in Paris in a semi-official capacity, but in reality he was no more than a spectre from a now vanished Russia. The reality was that the new, communist 'red' Russia and its leaders were the ones that had to be considered.

The war had unleashed many tensions, only some of which could be dealt with by the peace conference. Organized labour had been growing for decades in most countries, and its role had been crucial in the war effort. The rise of a communist regime in Russia, appealing directly for support to the workers was a further matter of concern. How to deal with the relationship between workers and employers and the setting of minimum standards had also become a pressing political matter.

Throughout January the delegates and their staffs were busy establishing contact with each other and attempting to make an initial assessment of each participants' views. The key figures at Paris were the leaders of the three major allied states, the American President Woodrow Wilson, the British Prime Minister, David Lloyd George, and the French premier, Georges Clemenceau, but there was also a host of equally talented leaders representing the smaller allies. Lloyd George later recalled, 'We were all feeling our way and I had a sense that we were each of us trying to size up our colleagues, reconnoitring their respective positions, ascertaining their aims and how they stood in reference to the desiderata in which each of them was most deeply interested and involved.'[2]

Lloyd George had risen from humble origins in his native Wales to become one of the longest serving senior government figures. An anti-war advocate during the Boer War he had later been one of the first to signal the growing security threat to British interests emanating from Germany. After the outbreak of war he became a brilliantly successful Minister of Munitions before becoming prime minister in 1916 and he was widely credited with overseeing a successful renewal of the British war effort. A Liberal, he led a coalition government and depended upon Conservative support. When the communist regime in Russia published late in 1917 a six-point proposal for a peace settlement based on no annexations or indemnities Lloyd George was quick to respond. In January 1918 he laid out his vision of the postwar order in what became known as the Caxton Hall speech [*Doc. 2*]. A few days later President Wilson added his own ideas in his Fourteen Points speech. At the conference Lloyd George was able to deploy his considerable charm, forensic talent and native guile to achieve British ends.

Clemenceau was nicknamed 'the tiger'. As a young man he had gone to the United States to fight upon the side of the North in the Civil War, arriving just as the war ended. He remained there for some years and became fluent in English, though at the conference he always insisted upon using French, thereby gaining some time as his English-speaking colleagues' remarks were translated for him. He had become premier in 1917, when it looked as though France might not be able to continue the war, and emerged as the architect of French victory. Having twice in his lifetime seen a German invasion of his country, he was determined to achieve a peace that would prevent such an event occurring again. Clemenceau, who prided himself on being a realist, was well aware of the importance of the peace negotiations. He remarked to a colleague late on the night of 11 November after the celebrations surrounding the end of four long years of war, 'we have won the war: now we have to win the peace, and it may be more difficult.'[3]

Wilson, a university professor and university president before entering politics, was an expert on constitutional practice. A fervent believer in democracy, he sought to extend to the international system the stability that constitutional mechanisms provided to the domestic affairs of democratic states. His pronouncements on the objects of the war and general ideas on the postwar order had led him to be revered as few leaders in history have been. Wilson's decision to attend the conference in person was precedent-shattering. He became the first American president to leave the United States during his term of office. Upon his arrival in Europe Wilson was viewed as a saviour by the great crowds who turned out to see him, his picture was placed in churches along with those of the saints and, on his railway journey from the port of Brest to Paris, people knelt by the tracks as he passed.

Wilson advocated a new approach to the handling of international affairs – the New Diplomacy. His plans for the postwar settlement spoke of an end of secret treaties, national and minority rights, and the creation of an international organization to assure international stability, an organization in which all states both great and small would be represented. Wilson had first presented his view of the postwar world in a landmark speech in January 1918, in which he enumerated fourteen points which could serve as the basis for a settlement [*Doc. 3*]. As the war went on he further elaborated his views in that statement, amounting to twenty-three major policy assertions by the eve of the peace conference. None of the other leaders had such a clearly articulated view of a new world order or one with such broad popular appeal.

Wilson, whose ideas were very much in the liberal tradition, argued that the war was being fought for the ideals of liberal democracy. Wilson took the view that nation-based states provided the best chance for stability, having concluded that the volatility of previous decades had been due to attempts by various national groups to assert their independent identities. Given the collapse of the old multi-ethnic eastern European empires, Wilson saw such a solution as the most likely to provide a stable structure for that region in particular.

In order for Wilson's plan to succeed, however, he had to take into account the fundamental concerns of the Allied states. The 'Fourteen Points' was a carefully crafted document that acknowledged basic Allied demands, such as the return of Alsace–Lorraine to France, without which the chief allied states were unlikely to agree to any settlement. The remainder of his framework was loosely worded in order to provide the flexibility necessary to determinine detail as circumstances evolved. For Wilson, though, it was clear that the key element of any postwar settlement was the creation of an international organization, the League of Nations, intended to provide the basis for a stable postwar order. The rationale behind such a development was not just an awareness of the crises which had led to this war, but also a concern about threats to international stability already looming in the immediate future. The Fourteen Points had a twofold aim: first, to produce the basis for a peace settlement and second, to provide an ideological alternative to Lenin and the Communist regime in Russia. The old European powers had eventually turned to Wilson's proposals both as a way to end the war and as a reason to stave off the communist threat to their own governments, and it was on the understanding that the final peace would follow the ideas of the fourteen points that the German government agreed to an armistice in November 1918.

America's European partners, however, were not enthusiastic about all of Wilson's plans. Clemenceau exclaimed in frustration of Wilson, 'He exasperates me with his fourteen commandments when the good God had only ten.'[4] Neither France nor Britain, which both possessed vast polyglot empires, were excited about national self-determination. Indeed Britain was facing immediate problems in Ireland, which had been in a state of simmering rebellion since 1916. Likewise, Wilson's denunciation of secret diplomacy and secret treaties was extremely awkward because the European Allies had, in their series of such secret wartime agreements, agreed in advance to the division between themselves of much of the German colonial and the Turkish Middle Eastern empires.

All states attending a conference have their own ambitions, and Paris was no different. At the heart of French plans was its security concerns about Germany, and the desire therefore to acquire as great a security buffer as possible. France also hoped that Germany would be forced to pay heavy financial penalties, which would not only assist the recovery of France's war-ravaged economy but would also act to cripple Germany for decades to come. The British, with an empire now spanning a quarter of the world, had a more complex set of concerns. In western Europe, Britain wished to see restored a balance of power that would prevent any one state dominating the region and, therefore, posing a security threat to Britain. In eastern Europe, Britain hoped to see a series of stable states emerge from the wreckage of the collapsed empires that had previously dominated the region, with the expectation that these would help maintain future stability in Europe. In the world beyond Europe Britain, which was in control of much of the territory formerly controlled by the Central Powers, was faced by a dilemma. Some old-style imperialists felt that Britain should keep everything it possibly could, others thought that Britain should take only a few key strategic locations, while yet another group was concerned that the British Empire was already greatly overextended and that it should keep as little as possible. One of the last group, Edwin Montagu, the Secretary of State for India, commented of the seemingly voracious appetites of the old-style imperialists, 'It would be very satisfactory if we could find some convincing argument for not annexing all the territories in the world.'[5] The United States had neither ambition nor need for territory or money. Wilson's central aim was the creation of a League of Nations, which he believed would help prevent future wars and begin to manufacture a more stable world order. All three powers saw the peace in differing ways; Wilson's was a long-term strategy that would take time to bear fruit, France's concerns were immediate, while British ambitions were medium term.

There were also a host of smaller states, some of which had been newly created out of the changes wrought by the war, clamouring for extensive territorial rearrangements in their favour. Particularly in eastern Europe many of these claims were overlapping, often based on historic grounds that did not always match the contemporary ethnic reality. Wilson had argued in his Four Principles that, 'Peoples and provinces must not be bartered about from sovereignty to sovereignty as if they were chattels or pawns in a game,' but that was just what some states wanted. One of the greatest problems the peacemakers would face was the determination of a new political map that would come as close as possible to creating nation-based states, particularly in eastern Europe with its patchwork quilt of nationalities.

Finding solutions to so many problems would tax the skills of those involved. One young Australian diplomat assigned to the British delegation, told his brother after six months of working on the settlement, 'One is always on the go and just on the brink of hope or despair.'[6] The scale of the upheavals to the ordinary lives of people, and of the wider international order brought about by the First World War, forms the backdrop to the continued efforts to reconstruct a stable international system during the years 1919–25. Those efforts began with the opening of the Paris Peace Conference on 18 January 1919.

Notes

1 H. Nicolson, *Peacemaking 1919* (London, 1933), p. 32.
2 D. Lloyd George, *The Truth About the Peace Treaties* (London, 1938), vol. I, p. 214.
3 D. Watson, *Clemenceau: a political biography* (London, 1974), p. 327.
4 H. Elcock, *Portrait of a Decision* (London, 1972), p. 33.

5 28 Dec. 1918. CAB 23/42/IWC44. Cabinet Papers, Public Record Office, London.
6 A.W.A. Leeper to R.W.A. Leeper, 5 June 1919. AWA Leeper Papers, Churchill College, Cambridge.

CHAPTER TWO

THE PARIS PEACE CONFERENCE AND THE VERSAILLES TREATY

THE PARIS PEACE CONFERENCE

The Paris Peace Conference opened with great ceremony on 18 January 1919, symbolically chosen as it was the anniversary of the proclamation of the German Empire in 1871. The venue was later criticized on the basis that the atmosphere in Paris, which was still highly charged from the toll of the war, helped to promote an unduly harsh settlement. Paris was chosen over other venues for several reasons: the Supreme War Council, which had overseen the Allied war effort, was already located just nearby at Versailles; possible neutral venues, such as Geneva, did not have the space; and Paris was the only city with the infrastructure to house such a vast gathering. It has been estimated that over 10,000 people were in Paris in connection with the conference, the American delegation alone numbered 1300, while in comparison Lord Castlereagh had taken only fourteen officials with him to the Congress of Vienna in 1814. The initial idea for the gathering at Paris was that it would provide an opportunity for the Allies to coordinate their negotiating plans ahead of peace talks with the Central Powers, and from January to March it was officially known as the Preliminary Conference of Peace. The rapid disintegration of the Central Powers in the weeks after the armistices, saw the Paris meeting seamlessly transform itself from a preliminary Allied gathering into the final peace conference. This explains one of the curiosities of the gathering – none of the Central Powers were invited to attend. Instead, all the negotiations were conducted among the Allies themselves and final treaties were presented to the defeated states.

The opening weeks of the conference were no more than the Indian summer of the wartime alliance, before the conflicting aspirations of its members would begin to drive them apart. The flurry that attended the opening of the long-awaited conference only marked the beginning of a long period of sluggish activity. From the outset the number of countries represented and the complexity of the issues to be resolved caused organizational difficulties. With thirty-two countries participating there were too many delegations for real work to be conducted in all-inclusive plenary sessions. Only six plenary sessions were held before the treaty with Germany was signed, and the only topic of substance discussed at these was the creation of the League of Nations. On 12 January 1919, just ahead of the official opening of the conference, the heads of the delegations of the major powers, Britain, France, Italy, and the United States met and agreed that decision-making on major issues would be kept in their hands, with the addition of Japan to the group. To facilitate this they established a Supreme Council, commonly called the Council of Ten, comprising the leaders and foreign ministers of Britain, France, Italy, the United States, and Japan. Even this proved too slow and cumbersome and in March it was superseded by a Council of Four, comprising the leaders of Britain, France, Italy, and the United States (Japan opted not to involve itself in primarily Eurocentric discussions). This new executive body was supplemented by a Council of Five to handle subsidiary questions, made up of the foreign ministers of Britain, France, Italy, the United States, and Japan. Some detailed work was given to special commissions in which the smaller powers participated. Even with such streamlining, differences between the chief allies were such that it was May before the proposed treaty was ready to be given to Germany. After the signature of the German peace treaty in June most of the major international leaders had to return home, and the final work of the conference was dealt with by a Conference of Ambassadors who finalized the details of the other four peace treaties along the lines of the German treaty. It was not until 1920 that the last of the peace treaties was signed and the work of the postwar peace negotiations completed.

The chief political figures at the conference were America's President Woodrow Wilson, the British prime minister David Lloyd George, and the French premier Georges Clemenceau. Each was assisted by teams of political and technical advisers. In the Fourteen Points Wilson had spoken of open covenants openly arrived at, and the horde of reporters who descended upon Paris expected to witness a new style of negotiation open to the public gaze. The realities of diplomacy, however, were that in the cut and thrust of negotiation the real talks would have to be held out of the public arena. Wilson insisted upon closed negotiations and it was Clemenceau, himself a former newspaperman, who won the case for the plenary negotiations to be made public, well aware that little of substance would occur there. As a result the general public was fed upon a diet of rumours and leaks from the conference, one of the factors which drove the leaders to shift the most critical negotiations from the leaky Council of Ten to the reasonably tight Council of Four.

One development of the conference was the emergence of English as a language of diplomacy. French had been the normal language of communication between states since the eighteenth century. Both Lloyd George and Wilson disputed France's expectation that French would be the official language of the conference (neither of them spoke French). As a result it was agreed that French and English would have equal currency, though in the event of a dispute about meaning the French text would be definitive. This became the practice of the League of Nations and remains that of the United Nations.

THE GERMAN PROBLEM

Just as the war with Germany had been the focal point of the First World War, so the settlement with Germany was the focal point of the peace settlement. The terms of the settlement with Germany were largely determined by the British, French and American leaders. Each of these three powers brought its own concerns to the settlement. For Clemenceau and France the chief desire was security against a future German attack. France, therefore, hoped to create a territorial buffer to act as a security cordon against Germany. Britain sought to restore a balance of power to western Europe that it saw as essential to blocking any threat to its own security from any overpowerful European state. Wilson desired that any settlement be in line with the principles of his Fourteen Points. The fourth key state, Italy, had no border with Germany and therefore no immediate ambitions against Germany. In any case its premier missed most of the sessions in which the German settlement was decided, having walked out in protest at the lack of support for Italy's grandiose territorial ambitions in the Adriatic and the Aegean regions.

Frontiers

In western Europe the event which underlay all negotiations was the collapse of German power. The French plans for achieving security had at their core regaining control of the region of Alsace–Lorraine, lost to Germany in 1871, but France also had ambitions to annex or control the small grand duchy of Luxembourg, the coal-rich German Saarland, the industrially important German Rhineland, and Belgium. This would significantly extend French borders and influence beyond its prewar frontiers and make France the predominant west European power. British policy rested on a traditional preference for supporting a balance of power in western Europe, with the aim of preventing any single power from dominating the region and thus posing a threat to Britain's security. French and British aims therefore seemed contradictory. Britain accepted France's insistence on regaining Alsace–Lorraine, but it was opposed to any wider extension of French power. Britain had no desire to see the German threat replaced by a French one. It should be remembered that for centuries France had been seen by Britain as its primary adversary. Britain and France had only come to a tentative alliance in 1904 in the face of the growing threat from Germany. With that threat removed much of the rationale for their alliance had disappeared. This situation illustrates the difficulty of keeping wartime alliances together in peacetime once the common adversary has been defeated.

The Allied leaders quickly agreed to France regaining Alsace–Lorraine, restoring the Franco-German border that had existed between 1815 and 1870. Clemenceau briefly and unsuccessfully attempted to gain the more generous 1814 borders. The chief problem with the western European settlement came over the future of the Rhineland, that area between the Rhine River and the French border. France had historically aspired to control this region, which it felt would complete its natural borders. The Rhineland, though, was thoroughly German and to annex it to France would violate Wilsonian principles. To circumvent this obstacle France tried to promote a separatist movement in the region, with the aim of creating a puppet state, or states, under the influence of France. Such moves attracted little local support. France saw control of the Rhineland as a necessary part of its security against Germany and therefore as one of its fundamental objectives, while for Britain there was the need to establish a balance of power, and for the United States this would be a test of the principles of the New Diplomacy. France's allies were aware that to obtain French support in the rest of the settlement France's primary objective of security against Germany would have to be met. Finding a way to balance these various aims became the key crisis of the conference.

The solution ultimately arrived at was to leave the Rhineland as part of Germany, but to make it a demilitarized zone in which Germany could not maintain or deploy its forces. This would meet France's demand for a greater security buffer with Germany, while not increasing French power and not violating the principles of the new diplomacy. French security concerns were to be further allayed by an Anglo-American guarantee to come to France's aid if it were once again attacked by Germany. This solution met the needs of all the participants, though as events proved the Rhineland was to remain a volatile factor in European affairs. When Wilson failed to win approval in the United States Senate for the agreements he had negotiated at Paris the security guarantee lapsed [*Doc. 17*]. This led to France renewing its interest in dominating the Rhineland, causing a series of further crises until 1925. In 1936 Hitler used the remilitarization of the Rhineland to test the Anglo-French resolve to maintain the Versailles system. Throughout all these Rhineland crises Britain remained consistent in offering no support to France.

France had also laid claim to the coal-rich Saar as compensation for the mines they claimed Germany had deliberately destroyed as they retreated during 1918. Lloyd George was sympathetic but here Wilson was adamant that an entirely German district could not be handed over. Eventually a solution was reached under which Germany ceded sovereignty of the Saar to the League of Nations and the ownership of the mines for fifteen years, after which the inhabitants would be consulted on whether or not they wished to return to German sovereignty. In 1935, after a plebiscite, the Saar's inhabitants opted to return to German rule.

A number of other territorial issues relating to Germany also confronted the peacemakers. In each of these, due to Wilson's insistence, some mechanism for considering the views of the inhabitants had to be provided. Varying methods were used in an effort to assign territory in line with the New Diplomacy. Belgium had laid claim to three small parcels of territory from Germany, Eupen, Malmédy, and Moresnet. In the first two special registers were set up for anyone to object to the transfer to Belgium, though few did so. Denmark, which had been neutral during the war, hoped to regain the ethnically Danish portion of Schleswig lost by war in 1864. Here the Danish government showed remarkable restraint, rejecting Allied overtures that they might regain all the lost territory, insisting that they only desired those areas where the inhabitants wished to be part of Denmark. One Danish delegate explained that in their view, 'The presence of even a German minority within our borders would mean chronic agitation, later perhaps civil war, and then probably another European conflagration.'[1] Schleswig was therefore divided into two zones and the inhabitants' views obtained by a plebiscite. As a result north Schleswig returned to Denmark and south Schleswig remained with Germany.

Greater problems were encountered in determining Germany's eastern frontiers. The new Polish government was claiming extensive boundaries which included many non-Polish districts. France supported these claims as it wanted a strong Poland to act as a pillar of its security system against Germany. Wilson, in his Fourteen Points, had supported the recreation of a Poland that would include all indisputably Polish areas and would have access to the sea. Britain, though, was concerned that a Poland that included too large a German minority would be a cause of future crises. The Allied leaders turned the matter over to a special committee, which reported in favour of giving Poland most of its ambitions. The committee proposed that Poland be assigned the districts of Allenstein and Marienwerder, the port city of Danzig (Gdansk), most of West Prussia, and mineral-rich Upper Silesia. Plebiscites were held in Allenstein and Marienwerder, and Upper Silesia. As a result the former opted to remain in Germany, while Upper Silesia was partitioned. Danzig, though mostly German, was vital to Poland as the port of the Vistula river valley; otherwise Poland would be virtually landlocked. As a solution Britain proposed that Danzig become a free city, under a League of Nations commissioner, governed by its own elected senate, with its foreign affairs handled by Poland and coming within the

Polish customs system. This solution was adopted, though Poland still wanted its own seaport, whatever special rights it was guaranteed in Danzig. The Allies therefore agreed to create what became known as the Polish Corridor, a narrow strip of land linking Poland to the Baltic Sea. As a result of these decisions the German province of East Prussia became geographically detached from the rest of Germany. The Polish Corridor remained an irritant in German-Polish relations for the next two decades. This attempt to balance the needs of Poland with those of the East Prussian Germans illustrates one of the many difficulties faced by the peacemakers.

Germany was also stripped of its overseas empire. During the war, in a series of secret treaties, the European allies had already made a preliminary distribution of these colonies. Wilson, however, was not in favour of the continuance of old-fashioned imperialism, a view clearly expressed in point five of his Fourteen Points. A solution was reached, initially suggested by Jan Smuts of South Africa, by which the German colonies would pass to the League of Nations and be administered by one of the members of the League as a 'mandate.' The mandatory power was obliged to report annually to the Council of the League. Under this arrangement Britain received control of German East Africa (Tanganyika); Belgium took control of Ruanda-Urundi (Rwanda and Burundi); Britain and France divided the Cameroons and Togoland, with the bulk going to France; South Africa received South-West Africa (Namibia); most of the German Pacific islands south of the equator were assigned to Australia, except German Samoa and Nauru which went to New Zealand; and the islands north of the equator went to Japan.

Reparations

The issue of reparations payments has generally been regarded as the most flawed part of the settlement. Two separate questions were involved in the discussions on the financial assessments to be levied against the Central Powers. First there was the question of reparation, which involved payment for losses of non-military property or of property lost through actions unacceptable to the laws of war. The second question concerned the imposition of an indemnity, which was simply a penalty imposed on the defeated powers for having waged war and lost. An indemnity had been imposed by Germany upon France at the end of the Franco-Prussian War in 1871, set at a high level with the hope that it would prevent any French resurgence for some years. To Germany's surprise France rapidly repaid this indemnity. France likewise planned to demand a heavy indemnity from Germany and, having learnt from its own experience, was determined that this would be pitched at a level that would cripple Germany for decades to come. There was great popular support, in the aftermath of such a brutal struggle, for punishing Germany. In Britain's 1918 election campaign Eric Geddes, a member of the government, made the famous promise that, 'The Germans, if this Government is returned, are going to pay every penny, they are going to be squeezed as a lemon is squeezed – until the pips squeak.'2 During that campaign Lloyd George had promised that Germany would pay for the cost of the war up to its capacity to do so, and many of his coalition partners were determined that a high sum would be imposed. Wilson, however, in the Fourteen Points had specifically ruled out any indemnity. There was nonetheless strong sentiment among the European allies that Germany should pay the full cost of the war and all participants at the Paris Peace Conference, except the United States, put forward such a claim. Ultimately, because of Wilson's objections, the idea of imposing an indemnity was dropped and attention came to focus on how high the reparations payments could be set.

Having failed to win the argument over an indemnity the British and French leaders next proposed that the definition of civilian damage include war pensions. This alone would probably double the final sum due by Germany. Wilson, to the surprise of many, agreed to this. Nonetheless, the exact final sum was still to be determined. As the negotiations played themselves out at Paris the reparations question came to be debated as part of the western European settlement. French claims to punitive reparations were part of France's bid for hegemony in western Europe and would help to weaken Germany's power in comparison to France. For the same reason that France wanted such a penalty, Britain began to back away from it. The linkage of economic consequences to future diplomatic development was only just coming to be seen as an integral part of statecraft. For those within the British delegation primarily engaged in the territorial settlement the perception of reparations as a serious problem grew slowly, as its impact on the continental balance became more evident. Assessing punitive reparations on Germany had been a popular domestic proposal that offered the illusion not only of punishment but also of less domestic financial strain. Some negotiators, though, sensed the danger that harsh reparations might weaken Germany to the extent that it would cease to be an effective counterweight against France, an eventuality which suited French, but not British, plans. The British Treasury adviser at Paris, J. M. Keynes, had already warned in December that France's demand for a huge indemnity was intended as the basis for its continued occupation and ultimate acquisition of the Rhineland. Keynes opposed heavy reparations on several grounds but he was also among the first to perceive the linkage between financial instability and the balance of power. Increasingly the concerns of Keynes and his Treasury colleagues over the future financial stability of Germany meshed with the worries of the territorial advisers over French aims and this brought about a shift of attitude at the highest level. As concerns grew in the British delegation about French aims so British thinking on reparations began to alter during the critical month of March, when the conference considered the linked issues of the Rhineland and reparations.

As Lloyd George became aware of the significance of the reparations question British policy began to change. The pivotal month of the conference was between 25 March and 22 April when negotiations almost collapsed over the question of reparations and the Rhineland. This period also saw a demonstrable shift in public opinion in Britain and Lloyd George's successful consolidation of his position in the House of Commons. Given the complexity of the task and the need to move expeditiously, many of the issues to be resolved were being negotiated in parallel by groups of officials, with the political leaders working to resolve conflicts as they arose. In March 1919, Lloyd George took his most senior advisors to the old French royal palace at Fontainebleau for a weekend to consider the current status of the peace talks. For the first time they stepped back and considered as a whole what had been accomplished. The result caused a dramatic shift in the British position on a number of matters. Their views were embodied in Lloyd George's Fontainebleau Memorandum of 25 March, which concluded that the envisaged settlement was of Carthaginian proportions, that it was probably unworkable in the short term and certainly in the long term [*Doc. 6*]. Therefore, in the territorial settlement, he opposed transferring more Germans from German rule than could be helped and, as to reparations, he argued that Germany could not be both crippled *and* expected to pay. As a former Chancellor of the Exchequer he had a good grasp of financial issues as well as their political ramifications.

The British attempt to avoid high reparations payments began on 28 March when they proposed separating the issues of what Germany owed and what it could pay. Lloyd George argued that if a single assessment was made, whatever sum was named, many people in Britain and France would consider it too small. The cause of moderation was aided by Wilson who, in exasperation with French demands, ordered his ship, *George Washington*, to Brest in readiness to depart. Though the theatrics of the Italians, who later tried to mimic Wilson's threatened walkout, were generally ignored, it was obvious that Wilson did not dabble in idle gestures. That same afternoon the French capitulated and agreed to a moderation of the reparations assessment. In the choice between winning on reparations and losing the American alliance there was no contest.

How Germany was to make these reparations proved difficult to resolve. The German central bank, the Reichsbank, held gold reserves of only 2.4 billion gold marks, far below any estimate of what the reparations bill would reach. Germany could, potentially, pay in the form of manufactured goods or labour to assist in reconstruction. The Allies held divided views on these possibilities as well. It was clear that the powerful trades unions in Belgium and France would not accept free labour payments, while Britain had no desire to see German goods taking its markets. Even how to determine a final sum proved impossible. It was finally agreed on 7 April to establish an inter-allied Reparations Commission to set the sum owed no later than May 1921. When Germany finally signed the peace treaty it would be signing a blank cheque. The treaty, however, already provided for numerous financial obligations on the part of Germany. It was to make initial payments commencing in August 1919 that would have amounted to 20 billion gold marks by May 1921 when the Reparations Commission was due to report. Part of the payments would be in kind; for example, Germany was committed to provide 38 million tons of coal per year for ten years. Other items in the long list of goods in kind to be surrendered ranged from cattle to fishing boats. Part of these payments were intended to begin to cover the cost of the army of occupation. The purpose behind collecting such high reparations from Germany differed with various delegations: to destroy Germany, to collect the money and goods and, in some cases, both.

War Guilt

Linked to the resolution of the reparations issue was the issue of war guilt. As part of the solution to the reparations debate the twin issues of Germany's liability to pay and its ability to pay were decoupled. The moral right to demand full reparation for all the costs caused by the war was to be based on what came to be called the War Guilt clause, Article 231 of the treaty, in which Germany accepted responsibility for the war. Article 232 went on to acknowledge that Germany did not have adequate resources to make complete reparation, but stated that Germany would have to pay for all damage done to civilians and their property [*Doc. 9*]. The concept of war guilt also led the framers of the treaty to consider who were the war criminals. The Allied leaders asked the Dutch to surrender the Kaiser to a special international tribunal of five judges to be provided by each of the chief Allied states to be tried for, 'a supreme offence against international morality and the sanctity of treaties.' The Dutch refused to recognize the right of the Allies to demand the extradition of the former German ruler, who remained in exile in the Netherlands until his death in 1941. The Allies also demanded the right to try other senior German statesmen and military figures, as well as those accused of specific crimes against civilians and prisoners of war. Although Germany signed the treaty, including the clauses relating to the trial by this international tribunal of suspected persons, Germany subsequently refused to hand over these individuals. A compromise was eventually reached whereby suspects would be tried by the German Supreme Court. Eventually, forty-six test cases were presented to Germany of which only twelve resulted in prosecution and, of these, only six in convictions with light sentences and no further cases were brought.

Military limitations

The victors agreed that Germany should in future possess no air force, poison gas, heavy artillery or a general staff, that its army be limited to 100,000 soldiers and its navy to six battleships and some smaller vessels. The German army's number of rifles, machine guns and rounds of ammunition were limited, and the production of military goods was restricted to specified factories which were subject to Allied supervision. Three inter-Allied commissions were established at Berlin to supervise the military, naval, and air restrictions. Germany was also to dismantle all its fortifications in the west. This was in line with the belief that the war had been caused by German aggression and that future peace would be assisted by limiting Germany to what was felt to be a force sufficient only for defence. Such reduction in German military power also provided further reassurance to France's security needs.

During the negotiations a division had developed among the Allies over whether the German military should be comprised of volunteers or conscripts. The French, who had traditionally maintained a conscript army, advocated a short-service conscript army in order to give the German army a more civilian character and thus be less likely to be used as a tool by those with militaristic intentions. The British and the Americans, who had traditionally maintained volunteer forces, advocated a long-service, volunteer army, on the grounds that that would limit the number of people with military training. The initial number of soldiers proposed for the German army was 200,000 but France objected that if this was a career force which could serve as the nucleus for a national army, those numbers would have to be reduced. The compromise reached was to have an army of 100,000 soldiers on long-term enlistments of twelve years. Although the argument that linked conscription to militarism was criticized by many, in the final settlement, in part due to British insistence on this point, anti-conscription clauses were written into the peace treaties with the defeated powers.

THE IMPACT IN GERMANY

Having hammered out the terms of the settlement among themselves, the Allies summoned the Germans in early May to receive the treaty. Germany had been in a state of political turmoil since the end of the war. Revolts had broken out across Germany as news spread that the government was seeking an armistice and, on 9 November, some of the revolutionaries proclaimed a republic. The same night Kaiser Wilhelm II fled the country, taking refuge in the Netherlands. A new regime under Friedrich Ebert emerged which was beset from adversaries on both sides of the political spectrum. In the months between the armistice and the presentation of the peace treaty it was primarily engaged in establishing both its authority and domestic order. A constituent assembly was elected in January 1919 to decide on the future government of the country. The assembly was forced to meet at Weimar, rather than Berlin, due to the unstable situation in the capital. Ebert was elected the first president of the new republic in February 1919. Many politicians wished to seize this opportunity to establish a liberal, democratic, state.

The new German leaders were horrified, therefore, when, in May 1919, the proposed peace treaty was presented to Germany. The perceived harshness of the treaty appalled the German delegates who saw the new Germany being punished for the transgressions of the old regime. The German delegation was not allowed to negotiate with the Allies, but only to submit points for clarification. The Germans attempted to delay matters in the hope of obtaining some concessions. The Allies, however, presented a final text on 16 June and informed Germany that it had seven days to agree or the armistice would end and the Allied forces would resume hostilities. Although the German army was now in no condition to halt such an attack, the German government could not bring itself to agree to the treaty and resigned. Great difficulty was encountered in attempting to form a new government, which was achieved with only one day to spare, and the German parliament voted to accept the treaty, with the exception of the war guilt clauses. In the meantime news arrived that the bulk of the German fleet, which had been interned since November 1918 at Scapa Flow, off the coast of Scotland, had been scuttled by its officers and crews. The German admiral responsible claimed later that he had assumed that the German government would not sign the treaty and that, as hostilities would be resumed, it was his duty to prevent the fleet falling into Allied hands. News of this, however, only hardened Allied attitudes and they rejected the German government's reservations, giving Germany twenty-four hours to agree or face renewed hostilities. With only ninety minutes to spare the German delegates based near Paris announced that Germany had agreed to the treaty. The peace treaty was signed on 28 June, the fifth anniversary of the event which had sparked the war – the assassination of the Archduke Franz Ferdinand. The site chosen for this event was the Hall of Mirrors of the Palace of Versailles, where in 1871, the victorious German leaders had proclaimed the German Empire [*Doc. 10*].

CONCLUSION

The Paris Peace Conference and the Treaty of Versailles proved to be only the first phase of attempts to reach a settlement to the myriad problems of international relations cast up by the First World War. It was concluded while the memories of that brutal conflict were still fresh and it is not surprising that the settlement imposed upon Germany contained harsh elements. Criticism of the treaty came swiftly. Notable among its critics was Keynes who resigned his Treasury job and published, in late 1919, *The Economic Consequences of the Peace*, which condemned the reparations clauses and predicted that they would only lead to greater instability through the problems it would cause in Germany and through attempts at enforcement of the reparations payments. In his passionately written critique Keynes warned that this harsh settlement would lead to 'a civil war between the forces of reaction and the despairing convulsions of revolution, before which the horrors of the later German war will fade into nothing, and which will destroy, whoever is victor, the civilisation and the progress of our generation.'[3] Later historians have disagreed with the view that the Versailles settlement was a Carthaginian peace. William Keylor has argued that Versailles, 'was far from a Carthaginian peace, compared not only with the fate of ancient Carthage itself but more recently with the brutal treatement of defeated Germany at the end of World War II in the form of both territorial amputations and reparations.'[4]

Controversy in America over the collective security provisions of the League of Nations would ultimately lead to the rejection of the treaty in the Senate and United States withdrawal from the structure Wilson had done so much to create (see Chapter 4). This in turn would lead to the Anglo-American guarantee of France's security becoming void, and cause France to embark on more robust measures to ensure its security from Germany which, in turn, would cause mounting tension in western Europe.

Despite its many critics, the Versailles settlement did produce some notable accomplishments. Greater efforts than ever before were made to adjust borders in accord with the wishes of the inhabitants of the districts affected. The League of Nations was born out of the Treaty of Versailles. Although the war guilt clauses were controversial at the time because of their linkage to reparations, it did mark a dramatic move forward in the concept of the accountability of leaders and officials should war crimes have been committed. Germany's colonies were removed, but not annexed by the victors. They were placed instead under the oversight of the League of Nations with the clear provision that they be administered for the benefit of the inhabitants with a goal of ultimate independence, a decision that foreshadows the beginning of decolonization.

Notes

1 S. Bonsal, *Suitors and Supplicants* (New York, 1946), p. 207.
2 *Cambridge Daily News*, 11 December 1918, reporting Geddes speaking at Cambridge, 9 December 1918.
3 J.M. Keynes, *The Economic Consequences of the Peace* (London, 1971), p. 170.
4 William Keylor, 'Versailles and International Diplomacy', in M. Boemke *et al.*, eds, *The treaty of Versailles: a reassessment after 75 years* (Cambridge, 1998), p. 505.

CHAPTER THREE

THE NEW EUROPE

In 1918 the old order in eastern and southeastern Europe shattered, one of the manifold consequences of the First World War. The situation in this region was entirely different from that in western Europe. Here there was no status quo but, rather, a fluid and increasingly volatile region with many new, nationally orientated, states with undefined frontiers. The toll of the war was colossal in terms of loss of life, damage to infrastructure and the destruction of long-established institutions. Some, though, saw the opportunity to build a better future on the ruins of the old, the opportunity of building a New Europe. The Czech leader, Thomas Masaryk, observed that Europe was now, 'a laboratory sitting atop a vast graveyard.'[1] The collapse of the German, Austro-Hungarian, Russian, and Ottoman Empires allowed the resurgence of nationalities previously subsumed in these larger entities. In the wake of the war new states emerged and others expanded their frontiers. The new states were Finland, Estonia, Latvia, Lithuania, Poland, Czechoslovakia, and Yugoslavia, while Roumania and Greece greatly expanded their territory. Austria and Hungary, now no longer the nuclei of the multi-ethnic Habsburg empire, separated and proclaimed themselves republics, though neither was reconciled to the loss to neighbouring states of territory that included their ethnic kinsmen.

The various Allied Powers each had their own objectives in this region. France, as a Continental power, was looking to lay the foundations of a new alliance among the emergent states as the basis for future security. This would replace its old alliance with Russia which had lapsed with the communist seizure of power in that country. The aim of such an alliance would be twofold; first, to act as a restraint on Germany and second, to provide a buffer against Soviet Russia. The United States had less direct interest in the region, though Wilson saw it as a proving ground for the efficacy of his ideas on national self-determination. Britain's chief concern was to avoid an unstable eastern Europe whose problems would have a dangerous ripple effect upon the stability of western Europe, where Britain's primary security interests were to be found. It was concerned that too many small and, therefore, weak states would be a cause of instability. Therefore it pushed for the creation of larger states, which would of necessity encompass smaller ethnic groups, whose rights were in turn to be protected by a series of minority treaties. None of the concerns of the Allied Powers on eastern Europe conflicted, though they came to similar conclusions for different reasons.

France wanted to see stronger states emerge in this region to counterbalance Germany, Wilson also saw the utility of this and encouraged the cooperation of different national groups, and Britain was likewise supportive since it was concerned that the new states be large enough to be stable and secure. The result was encouragement for the establishment of Czechoslovakia and Yugoslavia, each made up of related, but different, nationalities. Also receiving support were those states and nationalities that had sided with the Allies. Roumania and Greece received support for expansion to their biggest feasible extent. These border changes were made to the detriment of the defeated Central Power. Separate peace treaties were concluded with each of the defeated states, the Treaty of Saint-Germain with Austria, the Treaty of Trianon with Hungary, and the Treaty of Neuilly with Bulgaria.

THE DEFEATED CENTRAL POWERS

On 12 November a new regime in Vienna proclaimed itself the German Austrian republic, as part of the new German republic. There was general support for the union, or *Anschluss*, of this rump, German-speaking portion of the old Austro-Hungarian Empire with Germany. This would be entirely in accord with the idea of national self-determination and the move to states with a common ethnic identity. Such a union, however, would strengthen Germany just at the time the Allies were attempting to find ways to constrain its power in the future. As a result articles in both the treaties of Versailles and Saint-Germain specifically forbid any union of Germany and Austria. The new republic was even compelled to change its name from German Austria to Austria. The new Austrian government, led by Dr Karl Renner, tried unsuccessfully to argue that the new republic was as much a new state as any of the other new states in eastern Europe and that, as such, it should not be liable to pay reparations. Nonetheless, Austria and Hungary were both treated by the Allies as the successor states of the Austro-Hungarian Empire and were therefore liable for the empire's part in the war. The peace treaty with Austria, the Treaty of Saint-Germain, was signed on 10 September 1919. By its terms the new Republic of Austria retained only 27 per cent of imperial Austria, was limited to an army of 30,000, and was required to pay reparations. The clause forbidding an Austro-German union remained controversial until it was achieved by Hitler in 1938; but an independent Austria was restored in 1945.

There were a number of problems in demarcating the frontiers of this new Austria. The future Austro-Italian border had been one of the subjects of the wartime, secret Treaty of London in which Italy had been promised a frontier as far north as the Brenner Pass, far beyond any ethnic Italian area. Wilson's Fourteen Points, however, demanded that borders be defined as far as possible along the lines of nationality. Wilson, though, accepted the Italian argument that the Brenner Pass was a natural strategic frontier, and acquiesced in the incorporation into Italy of approximately 220,000–250,000 German-speaking people in the area south of the pass. Italy's acquisition of the Trentino, South Tyrol, and Istria completed the Italian *Risorgimento* begun in the Italian Wars of Unification.

The Peace Conference also detached a small strip of territory from western Hungary, which became the Austrian province of Burgenland. This action led to renewed tension between Austria and Hungary and some viewed this decision as intended to provide a cause of friction between the two former partners, thus preventing their becoming allies. Italy was looking to establish good relations with Hungary, largely out of concern that its own gains at the expense of Austria would lead to tense relations. Italy, therefore, pushed to have the Allies reconsider the Burgenland decision and a compromise was reached whereby a small area around the town of Sopron (Ödenburg) was returned to Hungary. On the new Austro-Yugoslav border fighting broke out over control of the Klagenfurt district, forcing the Allies to intervene to determine the issue by plebiscite. For voting purposes the area was divided into two zones: A in the southern and predominantly Slovene districts, and B in the northern and predominantly German-speaking districts. Zone A was to vote first, and if it opted for Austria then no vote need be taken in Zone B. To the surprise of many, the inhabitants of Zone A voted in favour of Austria. This illustrates the complexity of such issues, as people do not always decide their preferences purely on the basis of ethnic identity.

Five days after Austria had proclaimed itself a republic on 11 November, the Hungarian government, led by Count Károlyi, proclaimed Hungary a republic on 16 November. Although an armistice had been signed on 13 November 1918, with the French army in the Balkans commanded by General Franchet d'Esperey, Hungary's neighbours took this opportunity to secure their territorial aspirations. Transylvania was occupied and unilaterally annexed by Roumania on 11 January 1919. Serbia took control of the Bácska, Baranya and the western Banat on 24 November 1918. Czech and Slovak forces took control of Slovakia and part of Ruthenia. In the wake of its defeat in war and the partial dismemberment of the old Kingdom of Hungary, the political situation began to polarize. In March 1919 a communist government took power, led by Béla Kun. The Allies were unhappy at this potential spread of Soviet Russian influence into central Europe and were concerned that this could lead to communist seizures of power in other countries. A special mission was sent under General Smuts to try to negotiate with Kun, but no agreement could be reached. Roumania now saw the opportunity to gain further territory and its army again began to advance. Czechoslovakia soon after did the same. The Roumanian government hoped it would now enjoy the support of the Allied powers under the guise of combating the spread of communism. By July 1919 the Roumanian army was only 100 km from Budapest and there was the possibility that all Hungary might be occupied. This led to the collapse of the Hungarian communist regime on 1 August, followed by the unopposed occupation of Budapest by the Roumanian army. A series of weak transitional governments proved wholly unable to grapple with the situation. A counter-revolutionary militia led by Miklós Horthy, the last commander of the Habsburg navy, now began to assume control in unoccupied Hungary, unleashing a 'White Terror' in place of the previous communist 'Red Terror'.

The Allies tried to intervene to stabilize the situation in Hungary, sending as their emissary the British diplomat, Sir George Clerk. In return for promises from Horthy to introduce democratic reforms the Allies orchestrated the withdrawal of the Roumanian army from the Hungarian capital, issuing an ultimatum to Roumania on 15 November which brought about their evacuation of Budapest, though they did not finally leave Hungary until March 1920. Horthy and his forces thereupon entered Budapest and Horthy would remain the dominant figure in Hungarian political life until 1944. There was a strong movement for a restoration of the monarchy, though the monarchists were divided between a return of the Habsburgs and the selection of a new monarch. As a result, it was decided to appoint a regent until the matter could be resolved, with Admiral Horthy being elected regent of the re-established Kingdom of Hungary in March 1920. Hungary thus became a land-locked kingdom without a king, ruled by an admiral.

Having, at last, a clearly established regime with which to deal, the Allies rapidly moved to conclude a peace treaty with Hungary, the Treaty of Trianon, on 4 June 1920. By its terms Hungary lost 71 per cent of its territory and 60 per cent of its population, was limited to an army of 35,000, and had to pay reparations. As a result of the new borders Hungary, like Austria, lost its outlet to the sea. Resentment was caused by the fact that the new frontiers left 1.8 million Hungarians just outside the country, particularly in Transylvania which was assigned to Roumania. Over 350,000 ethnic Hungarians fled to Hungary from the lost lands, further straining the domestic political situation. The chief aim of Hungary's alliance with Hitler in the 1930s was to regain these lands and peoples, which was temporarily achieved by the Vienna Awards (1938 and 1940).

The peace treaty with Bulgaria, the Treaty of Neuilly, was signed on 27 November 1919. By its terms Bulgaria lost the Southern Dobrudja to Roumania, four small but strategic salients on its frontier with Yugoslavia, its Aegean coastline, won only in 1913 in the Balkan Wars, was ceded to Greece. Bulgaria was limited to an army of 33,000 and was to pay reparations. In 1923 the financially stricken country's payments were cut from £90,000,000 to £22,500,000.

THE VICTOR STATES

Framing peace treaties with the defeated states proved difficult enough, but the problems were exacerbated by the ambitions of some of the victors and the newly emergent states, which were themselves often contradictory. Italy had entered both the war and the peace negotiations with exorbitant expectations of the rewards it would receive. It hoped to make the Adriatic into an Italian sea, but the creation of a large unified Yugoslavia was to prove an obstacle to this objective. Italy had entered the war after having received the commitment of Britain and France, in the secret 1915 Treaty of London, that it would receive the Trentino, Trieste, the south Tyrol to the Brenner pass, the Istrian peninsula, and northern Dalmatia. This would give Italy a strongly defensible northern border and extend its control over significant areas of the land lying opposite Italy across the northern Adriatic Sea. This brought Italy into confrontation not only with Yugoslav ambitions, but also with the views of Wilson. The American president had always made clear that he would not be bound by any of the commitments the Allies had made secretly between themselves before the United States became a partner to the war.

Italian forces had already occupied the Trentino and the important port of Trieste. The first possible crisis came over pushing Italy's border as far as the Brenner Pass, as this would include primarily German-speaking districts of the south Tyrol. Here Wilson made an early concession to Italy which conflicted with Point Nine of his Fourteen Points [*Doc. 3*]. Although he had called for Italy's borders to be readjusted along ethnic lines which, conceivably would have met most of its aspirations, he agreed early on that this could be adjusted to include the areas up to the Brenner Pass. This would create, he accepted, a secure border which, it was hoped, would assist in ensuring future security. The cost of this, however, was to leave 250,000 German speakers under Italian sovereignty. Wilson would later regret this action.

As the conference proceeded Wilson, while accepting most of Italy's other claims, did not accept its claim to Dalmatia, which was almost entirely Slavic. The Italian leaders then exacerbated the situation by adding a new claim to the port city of Fiume (Rijeka), until recently one of the chief ports of the Austro-Hungarian Empire. This city, with its mixed population, was claimed both by Italy and Yugoslavia: the old city having an Italian population and the outer districts and the hinterland a Slovene majority. As a port for all the countries in the region it was of great importance. Indeed, until this period, it had served as the chief port for the Hungarian portion of the Habsburg empire. Fiume lay well beyond the generous frontiers promised to Italy in the Secret Treaties and Wilson, having agreed to Italy's claims for the Brenner Pass frontier, was unwilling to agree to further bending of his basic principles. Britain and France felt some obligation to support Italian claims arising from the London treaty, although Fiume had not been explicitly mentioned. In an interesting contradiction, Italy was now claiming the Brenner pass frontier, on the basis of commitments made through secret treaties, and Fiume on the basis of Wilson's new open diplomacy and the principles of ethnicity. In fact, the Italian government was divided between those who saw Fiume as an unnecessary diversion when the object should be the acquisition of the important Dalmatian bases that would give Italy control of the Adriatic, and those who focused on bringing all Italians under one state. The foreign minister, Sidney Sonnino, saw the Adriatic as *Il Golfo,* and control of it as in the days of Venetian empire as essential to Italian security. These linked issues provide an example of some of the difficult contradictions often confronted by states seeking to achieve wide objectives.

The Allies occupied Fiume pending a final decision on its fate. Wilson reacted forcibly to what he saw as grasping demands by Italy's delegates and, using what he saw as a tool of open diplomacy, published his arguments in a leading newspaper. The Italian delegation reacted by walking out of the conference and returning home, where it was met by a popular reception. Wilson, briefly revered in Italy, was now reviled. The action of the Italian delegation, while wonderfully theatrical, did nothing to promote its real objectives. Despite Italy's absence, the rest of the conference proceeded and, as a result, Italy was not able to make its voice heard in many aspects of the wider settlement and, therefore, failed to influence many final conclusions. One example is that Italy, in the end, received none of the mandates to control former German or Ottoman territories which had been among its goals.

In part due to this crisis, the government of Orlando fell and he was replaced in June 1919 by Nitti, who had little more success. The Fiume issue continued unresolved. The situation changed dramatically, however, when on 12 September 1919 a group of Italians occupied Fiume, led by the eccentric poet d'Annunzio. The issue was left to smoulder for a period as other events captured the attention of the key powers. Ultimately, it was agreed that Fiume should become a Free City under the League of Nations. D'Annunzio, however, rejected this solution and, in a typically flamboyant gesture, he even declared war upon Italy. The dispute was ultimately resolved in a 1920 bilateral treaty by which Italy gained the port of Zara on the east coast of the Adriatic, a few islands, and most of the Istrian peninsula, although most of its population was Slavic. Fiume, following the model of the solution to the Danzig crisis, was to become a Free City. D'Annunzio refused to accept this solution and had to be removed by force by the Italians in January 1921. Fiume now entered a brief existence as a Free City, until 1922 when it was occupied by Italian forces. In 1924 Italy and Yugoslavia agreed by treaty that Fiume would become part of Italy, with the predominantly Slovene suburbs going to Yugoslavia. After the Second World War the areas gained by Italy in this dispute were all taken by Yugoslavia. Domestically, for Italy, the Fiume incident was also important because it showed the ability of dissident forces to defy the government. It helped convince many that Italy was being robbed of its rightful share of the spoils of war and thus contributed to the collapse of Italy's liberal democracy and the rise of a fascist regime under Mussolini in 1922.

Italian intransigence spawned a number of imitators, in particular Roumania which hoped to achieve the creation of a Greater Roumania. The difficulty was that the irredenta of the nascent Yugoslavia and the prospective Roumania overlapped. This resulted in the Italians backing the Roumanians on the principle of troubling the Yugoslavs, while the French backed the Yugoslavs, probably in order to irritate the Italians. Although Roumania's record during the war had been mixed, its forces acted effectively once the main hostilities had ended. Despite the existence of an armistice, Roumanian forces seized most of its desired territory from Hungary. The collapse of Russian power had also allowed Roumania to regain Bessarabia, a much-disputed district lying between the Pruth and Dniester rivers (which has changed sovereignty six times during the nineteenth and twentieth centuries). Not surprisingly, the regime in Moscow refused to recognize this and, given Roumania's diplomatic troublesomeness, the Allied powers were equally reluctant. Roumania began to follow a more constructive approach in early 1920, but an agreement recognizing Roumanian sovereignty over Bessarabia was accepted only by Britain. Diplomatically isolated and therefore possibly militarily exposed, Roumania now began to seek a stronger security arrangement, starting first of all with potential regional allies. This was one of the factors which led to the formation of the Little Entente, which would come to involve France as well.

The cause of South Slav unification had been one of the origins of the First World War and the motivation behind the assassination of the Archduke Franz Ferdinand, which had sparked the conflict. With the ending of the war the union of the South Slavs in the new Yugoslav kingdom (officially called at first the Kingdom of the Serbs, Croats, and Slovenes) was now a reality, but a reality without definite frontiers. While most of its borders were agreed by 1920, the final frontiers were not defined until 1924 when Yugoslavia abandoned its claim to the port city of Fiume. The new state incorporated the former Kingdom of Serbia, with its king assuming the new crown; the former Kingdom of Montenegro, whose own dynasty was deposed; the former Hungarian province of Croatia and the former Austrian province of Dalmatia, whose majority population were Croats; the former Austrian province of Carniola, and some other small parcels of territory which were primarily populated by Slovenes; the former Hungarian territories of Bácska, Baranya and the western Banat which had a mixed ethnic population; and Bosnia-Hercegovina, which had been under joint Austro-Hungarian rule and was comprised of Serbs, Croats, and Muslims.

POLAND

With the collapse of the empires at the end of the First World War, Poland re-emerged as an independent state, but without clear frontiers [*Doc. 11*]. The first president of Poland, Pilsudski, had himself been born in neighbouring Lithuania and dreamt of recreating the vast Polish-Lithuanian commonwealth, that had also covered much of the Ukraine during its fifteenth-century apogee. The attempt to define its borders would lead to six concurrent wars during 1918–21. The first was the Ukrainian war against the West Ukrainian republic that had taken power in what the Poles considered to be eastern Galicia, in territory that had been part of the Austro-Hungarian Empire. This republic hoped, ultimately, to join with the eastern Ukrainian state that had been part of the Russian empire. By July 1919 Poland had overrun this area and simply presented a fait accompli to the Allied powers. It had skirmishes with Germany over Posnan at the end of 1918, and there were three periods of conflict over Silesia from the summer of 1919 to 1921. Poland also fought a war with Lithuania over control of the city of Vilnius (Wilno) which Lithuania hoped to make its capital. Poland's success in this war embittered Polish-Lithuanian relations throughout the interwar period.

   A further conflict with far-reaching implications was the struggle with Czechoslovakia for control of the former Duchy of Teschen. This was a mineral-rich district that was also an important transportation centre. At the end of the war Poland and Czechoslovakia had agreed to delineate the border by amicable negotiation and, in the meantime, control was divided. In late 1918, however, Poland mobilized its army in the area and moved to incorporate the portions it controlled. In response, Czechoslovakia deployed its forces and skirmishing followed. The Allied great powers intervened and forced an armistice. Tensions in the district were so high that it was impossible to hold a plebiscite to determine the inhabitants' wishes and instead the Allied powers imposed a solution that left Czechoslovakia with the bigger portion but gave the city of Teschen itself to Poland. This conflict condemned the two countries to poor relations in the years ahead and when Hitler moved against Czechoslovakia in 1938, at the time of the Munich Crisis, Poland took the opportunity to seize the whole of Teschen, rather than make common cause against the threat being posed by Germany. At the time, Poland probably would have pursued its claims to Teschen but it was forced to accept the Allies' settlement as at the same time a large Soviet army was heading for Warsaw.

The biggest conflict came with Soviet Russia. The Paris Peace Conference proposed for Poland's eastern frontier a line, known as the Curzon Line, which included within Poland all those districts of a definitely Polish character. The Polish government, however, claimed a frontier much further east on historical grounds. The German evacuation of the contested district that lay between the Curzon Line and Poland's preferred eastern border, combined with Russia's distraction in a civil war, provided an opportunity for Poland to implement its claims. The Russians also attempted to occupy the evacuated districts and hostilities followed. The war began well for the Poles who, under Pilsudski, occupied the Ukrainian capital, Kiev, before a Russian counter-attack drove them back to the outskirts of Warsaw. In the Battle of Warsaw the westward advance of the Russian army was checked and the Soviet army driven back. By the Treaty of Riga in 1921 Poland received a frontier substantially to the east of the Curzon Line (see Chapter 5).

THE LITTLE ENTENTE

A web of alliances began to emerge among the eastern European states which came to be known as the Little Entente. It was a term first used derisively by a Hungarian journalist, recalling the prewar great power Triple Entente. Whereas that combination had been aimed against Germany, this new grouping was aimed against Hungary. Many of these new states were concerned that Hungary would make a bid to regain at least some of the vast territory it had lost. In December 1919 the Czechoslovak foreign minister, Beneš, proposed a mutual defence agreement with Yugoslavia against a Hungarian attack. The following month he extended the same invitation to Roumania. The Czechoslovak-Yugoslav pact was concluded in August 1920 [*Doc. 12*]. Roumania hesitated about joining but an abortive attempt by the deposed Habsburg emperor, Karl, to regain the throne of Hungary in early 1921, hastened the growth of the Little Entente. Within weeks Romania had agreed its own alliance with both Czechoslovakia and

Yugoslavia, in this case extended to cover the eventuality of an attack by Bulgaria. Over the next months and years this trilateral arrangement would be strengthened by military conventions and greater cooperation in foreign policy and trade matters. After 1926 the Little Entente states normally occupied (by rotation) one of the non-permanent seats on the League of Nations Council. These agreements were consolidated by the Treaty of Belgrade in 1929 which converted these alliances into an international organization with a permanent council and a secretariat.

The Little Entente came into being without direct French assistance, but it sat well with French thinking. France, until the First World War, had based its security against Germany on an alliance with Russia. With the Russian revolution France lost this partnership and sought to replace it with a network of arrangements with the newly emergent eastern European states. France promoted its own security structure in eastern Europe as a parallel and separate arrangement outside whatever security would be provided by the new and untried League of Nations. It therefore put its hopes in the mechanisms of the new diplomacy and insured itself with the traditonal mechanisms of the old diplomacy. France began to build its own bilateral ties with the Little Entente states, starting in 1924 with a treaty of alliance with Czechoslovakia [*Doc. 16*]. The pivot of French plans at this time, however, was Poland which it supported during its war with Soviet Russia and with which it concluded a treaty of alliance in 1920. It was estimated that Poland would be able to raise an army of four million soldiers, making it a valuable military ally against any renewed German aggression. It proved impossible to bring Poland into the Little Entente, however, because of the poor state of Czechoslovak-Polish relations that had arisen over the struggle for the control of Teschen. This weakness in the security structure in eastern Europe would later help prevent cooperation against Hitler's Germany.

THE MINORITY PROTECTION TREATIES

Given the ethnic complexity of eastern Europe, it was impossible to draw frontiers which did not leave minority populations. Therefore fourteen states were required to sign special minority rights treaties or make similar declarations to the League of Nations (Finland, Estonia, Latvia, Lithuania, Poland, Czechoslovakia, Austria, Hungary, Roumania, Yugoslavia, Albania, Greece, Turkey, and Iraq). All these states complained that the great powers were not required to agree to similar provisions. Wilson, though, argued that the Peace Conference was attempting to eliminate as far as possible sources of potential disturbance. While the Great Powers were attempting to arrange an equitable distribution of territory, the reality of minority populations left a possible source of later upheaval. Therefore it was necessary to do everything possible to ensure that minorities would not feel unjustly treated.

Europe was familiar with the problem of the transfer of populations from one state's sovereignty to that of another. Earlier major peace settlements had contained provisions to safeguard the rights of populations so transferred, notably that reached at Vienna (1814), Paris (1856) and Berlin (1878). The Berlin settlement had extended the principle even further, with the various Balkan states having to agree to protect their Muslim populations, while the Ottoman Empire pledged to protect its Christian subjects. None of these agreements, however, contained any mechanism for enforcement. The Paris Peace Conference not only extended the principle of protection to cover all minorities in the states adhering to such arrangements, but also provided a mechanism of appeal to an international body.

The problem of how to protect minority rights was one of the many conundrums facing the peacemakers. A Committee on New States was established which ultimately produced, as the best solution for this problem, a basic template for a minorities protection treaty. By internationalizing the issue through specific treaty obligations, rather than relying on mere principles to be declared through the League of Nations, a major, if at the time not so noticed, leap was made in international governance. The first agreement was signed with Poland, on the same day that the German peace treaty was signed at Versailles. All the minority protection treaties followed a similar formula. The treaties contained a general statement of underlying principles and specifics on the granting of citizenship, aimed at preventing discrimination against the minorities. Most importantly it contained the mechanics of enforcement. It was usually the practice that members of minority groups could appeal to the League of Nations, which established a special Minorities Commission. Differences of opinion would be adjudicated by the new Permanent Court of International Justice, whose decision was to be binding. One of the leading historians on this issue, Carole Fink, has observed that, 'The weary victors hesitated to confer on minorities too prominent a status, weaken the new governments, or provide minority defenders with the means to dispute the new order.'[2] Although the effectiveness of these minority protection agreements varied from state to state, it was a significant step forward in the recognition of human rights.

CONCLUSION

The treaties of Saint-Germain, Trianon, and Neuilly with the defeated Central Powers have often been criticized for creating so many minority problems. In retrospect the number of geographical decisions that had to be made in creating a new political landscape may seem bewildering, but they were just as much so to the peacemakers at the time. In a world exhausted by war, with small conflicts still raging in the region and the need to establish governments with clear authority over clearly demarcated states, with time of the essence for fear that order would break down altogether and concerned about the possible spread of Soviet Russian power, the peacemakers laboured to establish an effective settlement. The reality of the patchwork of national population distribution made it impossible to draw neat frontiers which left no minorities. It did, nonetheless, leave three times as many people free from alien rule as were left subjected to it. The minority protection treaty system was not without its flaws, but for the first time the international system had not only evolved a concept of minority civil rights, but had attempted to find a way to enforce it. Nonetheless, the settlement that evolved for the new Europe was untested and, as Masaryk had observed, it was still a laboratory.

Notes

1 M. Baumont, *La Faillite de la paix, 1918–1939* (Paris, 1946), p. 8.
2 Carole Fink, 'The Minorities Question at the Paris Peace Conference: The Polish Minority Treaty, June 28, 1919', in M. Boemke *et al.*, eds, *The treaty of Versailles: a reassessment after 75 years* (Cambridge, 1998), p. 274.

CHAPTER FOUR

THE LEAGUE OF NATIONS

The horrors and vast scale of the First World War spurred the development of ideas for ways to prevent the recurrence of conflict. Interest in some form of general international organization had been discussed by several generations of publicists.[1] The collapse of the old concert system, combined with hopes of creating lasting peace and security, now impelled the Allied powers to convert these proposals into policy. By the time the Armistice was signed it was clear that the creation of a League of Nations would be part of any peace settlement. Woodrow Wilson had called for such an organization in the Fourteen Points [*Doc. 3*], as had Lloyd George in his Caxton Hall speech of January 1918 [*Doc. 2*] when he declared the creation of a similar body as being among Britain's three preconditions for establishing a permanent peace. The French government had also been working on plans for an international organization.

The concept of a League of Nations grew out of several earlier developments. In the seventeenth and eighteenth centuries philosophers such as William Penn and Emmanuel Kant, among others, had proposed schemes for perpetual peace. The nineteenth century saw substantive steps to promote international peace, one of which was the search for mechanisms to prevent war. This effort reached a critical stage at the Hague conferences of 1899 and 1907, which sought to establish judicial mechanisms for resolving conflict. A second step was the growth of international organizations that promoted international cooperation, beginning with the Universal Postal Union in 1875. While non-political, they provided evidence of the efficacy of international cooperation. The Allied experience of wartime cooperation through joint Allied commissions controlling raw materials, shipping and trade provided further evidence of the utility of cooperation. An added factor was that many blamed the secret diplomacy of the prewar era for the drift to war and Wilson had proposed that the solution to this was Open Diplomacy. It was envisaged that the League would provide a forum for such open diplomacy, where all treaties and agreements between states would be deposited and published. During the war public pressure groups emerged to support the idea, such as the League to Enforce Peace in the United States and the League of Nations Society in Britain.

THE PEACE CONFERENCE

All the major powers had been evolving plans for this new international organization. Léon Bourgeois of France had been working on such ideas for many years and, in 1917, became head of a French government committee to draw up a firm proposal. The French plan called for a much stronger League than that envisaged by the other powers, with mandatory membership and a requirement for all members to participate in implementing League decisions, where necessary, through the use of military, naval, and economic means. France saw the League as providing for mutual defence through a common military force with its own staff, similar to the Allies' Supreme War Council that had provided for unity of planning and control during the war. Much of this scheme was perceived by the other states as a means to help assure French security in the event of any renewed German aggression (France proposed that the League military force be based on its frontier with Germany), and it attracted little support.

In the final design of the League of Nations British ideas were particularly influential. British efforts to study how to implement the general concept of an association of nations began in earnest immediately after Lloyd George's Caxton Hall speech, with the establishment of a committee under Lord Phillimore, a noted jurist. Among the more significant recommendations of the Phillimore Committee was that force in the form of military and economic sanctions should be used if necessary to bring disputing states to international arbitration. Such states would be bound to attempt reconciliation, which naturally meant delay and which it was hoped would allow passions to cool. It was when states avoided this process that the other members of the system would drag them into a conference to settle the matter. It was also proposed that the members bind themselves not to go to war with each other, to use arbitration and, in the last resort, for members to go to war with a state which refused arbitration. The procedure for arbitration was an ad hoc affair, resembling the ambassadors' conferences of the prewar order. The Phillimore proposals did not go as far as later plans, which called for an organization with a full-time staff located at a permanent headquarters. Rather, the Phillimore Committee supported the creation of an agreed machinery to be activated in times of international stress.

These ideas were further developed in two reports by Foreign Office experts, which appeared in November 1918. The first, by Lord Eustace Percy, recommended that Britain should support the formation of a League of Nations that would promote regular, international consultation and that would have a permanent, international secretariat. While the original members would be the Allied powers, Percy considered that the new states of Europe and the neutrals should be invited to join. This new league would act as guarantor of the whole peace settlement and of the political and territorial integrity of its members. Percy envisaged this guarantee as being both collective and individual, thus allowing room for states to exercise independent judgement. He proposed that Britain should put forward the Phillimore Committee's report as the best scheme for the peaceful settle-ment of disputes. Percy believed it to be advisable to concentrate first on establishing a league along these lines, while leaving such volatile and potentially divisive issues as disarmament, freedom of the seas, and equality of trade conditions for future consideration. If too many issues were thrust upon the league at birth, he feared that it would be unable to cope.

Percy's report was supplemented by one by Alfred Zimmern that followed a similar line in recommending a permanent organization charged with arranging regular conferences. He suggested, however, that, while the League's guarantee of peace should be permanent, it would be wiser if all other treaties were not concluded for a duration exceeding ten years, when they could be renewed. He argued that long-term treaties were not consistent with the principles of state sovereignty. Zimmern, Percy, and the Phillimore Committee all concurred that the coercive power of the League should be limited to occasions when arbitration had either been refused or an arbitral award ignored.

Lord Robert Cecil, a junior minister in the government, had long been interested in the idea of a League of Nations and, in December, he submitted his own scheme for such an organization. The Cecil Plan synthesized the common points of the earlier proposals, with regular conferences acting as the pivot of the League's activities. Cecil went a step further than the earlier proposals in suggesting that the League should have an independent capital, with a chancellor as its chief executive officer.

The most notable contribution from Britain, though, was made by Jan Smuts, the South African statesman placed in charge of British preparations for the peace conference by Lloyd George. Smuts argued that the ordinary conception of the League of Nations was not a fruitful one and that a radical transformation was required. He observed that with the destruction of the old European empires and the passing of the old European order a vacuum had been created which could only be successfully filled by a powerful league. He did not perceive such an organization as acting only to help in the prevention of wars, but rather as something that would play an integral part in the ordinary peaceful existence of people. The experience the Allies had already gained during the war in cooperating on the control and rationing of food and raw materials provided a useful precedent that could be used to extend economic cooperation through the League in peacetime.

Smuts firmly opposed a peace of annexations and he proposed that all territories surrendered by the defeated states, not yet considered ready for self-government, should be placed under the supervision of the League. The Great Powers would assist in the development of the regions formerly under Russian, Habsburg, and Ottoman rule. Smuts did not exclude Germany from participating in this work, once stability had been restored in that country. His plan would have given the Great Powers extensive control in eastern Europe, Siberia, and Western Asia.

Smuts's proposals on the organization of a League drew heavily on his experiences of the relationship between Great Britain and the Dominions. His aim was neither to create a super-state, nor simply to establish an office for organizing conferences. Smuts wanted an organization of sufficient suppleness and flexibility to be able to adapt to the evolving needs of the international system. He proposed that the League have a two-tier system, comprising a council and a general conference. He agreed with the earlier proposals for a secretariat, and for the settlement of disputes along the lines suggested by the Phillimore Committee. War was not outlawed, but the system would do everything possible to prevent it by delay and arbitration.

The council was to be the permanent nucleus of the League, which would supervise the variety of tasks with which Smuts hoped the League would be charged. Smuts introduced an innovation by suggesting that the council be comprised of two classes of members. The Great Powers would sit as permanent members while the remaining states would be classified as intermediate and minor powers, each group being allowed two seats on the Council by rotation. Three adverse votes would be sufficient to defeat a resolution. The lower tier of this system was a General Conference that would meet periodically. Smuts concluded his proposals by focusing on what he perceived as the cause of militarism, which the League could assist in eliminating. He called for the abolition of conscription, the limitation of armaments, and the nationalization of armaments production with League inspection. Much of what Smuts proposed was based on the conclusions of the Phillimore, Zimmern, and Percy plans, modified by several further suggestions, and has remained a part of modern international organizations. The British government decided to try to achieve the creation of a League of Nations along the lines proposed by these schemes, and at Paris this early work played an important role in the shaping of this innovation in the development of the international system.

Wilson did not himself set out definite plans for a League, but rather arrived at the peace conference intending to place the drafting of a plan of organization for the League of Nations ahead of other work, before it could be shunted aside by the more technical details of peacemaking. Wilson was aware that there would be imperfections in any settlement and envisaged one of the purposes of the League would be to act as a mechanism for subsequent adjustment of imperfections, as well as for enforcing the terms of the peace. Wilson had been kept informed of British ideas on the subject and had integrated many of those ideas into his own thinking as it evolved.

A draft plan was worked out by the British and American legal advisers, the Hurst–Miller plan, which took into account Wilson's basic premise and the most favoured ideas that had developed out of the British process. This draft formed the basis for negotiations between all the allies at Paris, and was substantially the basis for the final constitution of the League of Nations, the Covenant, which was incorporated into the peace treaties with Germany, Austria, Bulgaria, and Hungary. As a result, the League did not formally come into being until the first treaty came into effect in January 1920.

The Covenant consisted of twenty-six articles. Articles 1–7 dealt with issues of membership; Articles 8–9 with disarmament and arms control; Article 10 promised mutual respect for other members' territorial integrity and political independence and for joint protection from external aggression [*Doc. 8*]; Article 11 allowed members to appeal to the Council to discuss disputes [*Doc. 8*]; Articles 12–15 dealt with methods for resolving disputes; Article 16 obligated members to take prompt action against any member which went to war in violation of the Covenant and gave the Council the power to expel erring states; Article 17 gave members the same protection against non-members as agreed in the Covenant; Articles 18–21 concerned the impact of the Covenant on other treaties and for the publication of all treaties; Article 22 established the mandates system; Articles 23–25 concerned the League's desire to improve international cooperation in areas of mutual concern which would be accomplished through the establishment of various subsidiary bodies and for bringing within the League structure existing bodies; and Article 26 provided provisions for amending the Covenant.

WILSON, UNITED STATES REJECTION, AND ARTICLE 10

With the signing of the Treaty of Versailles, which included the covenant, this phase of the peace settlement was concluded and President Wilson returned to the United States, where he encountered growing opposition to the treaty. The Republicans, who formed a majority of 49 to 47 in the Senate (where the treaty required a two-thirds vote for ratification), were generally negative about the treaty. Wilson had insisted of the Allies that the Covenant of the new League of Nations be incorporated as an integral part of the peace treaty. The Republican opposition was led by Senator Henry Cabot Lodge, the chairman of the powerful Senate Foreign Relations Committee. Opposition focused on what were perceived as infringements of the Monroe Doctrine, widely seen as encapsulating the fundamental necessities of American foreign policy. Already in March 1919, after a brief mid-conference visit to Washington, Wilson had agreed to move to amend the Covenant to address these concerns, clarifying that domestic issues such as immigration and tariffs were exempt from the purview of the League, and adding provisions for withdrawal. After some difficulties with the Allied leaders Wilson's desired modifications were made.

Wilson's modifications, however, were not enough to assuage his opponents who, upon his return, launched a political offensive against the Covenant. In a desperate gamble Wilson took his case directly to the people, crossing the country in a remarkable campaign to enlist popular support. On 25 September 1919, in the midst of this campaign Wilson suffered a debilitating stroke at Pueblo, Colorado, from which he never fully recovered. The Republicans continued to argue that the treaty should only be ratified if there were clear reservations as to its applicability to the United States. Once again, Wilson was willing to agree to many of these, and he and Lodge were not, in fact, far apart in what they would accept. What Wilson refused to give way on was Article 10 of the Covenant, which committed members to preserve the territorial integrity of other states from external aggression [*Doc. 8*]. The result was the defeat of the treaty in the Senate on 19 November 1919, and with it United States membership in the League of Nations. It was left to Wilson's successor as president, Warren Harding, to conclude a formal peace with Germany and the other Central Powers with which the United States had been at war. Only on 2 July 1921 did the United States formally declare an end to hostilities and in August 1921 it signed peace treaties with Germany, Austria, and Hungary which ensured it the benefits received by the Allied states, without any of the obligations.

Article 10 lay at the heart of the debate in the United States over membership of the League of Nations. This was the clause by which members agreed to preserve the territorial integrity and independence of all members. France had initially hoped this would take the form of a League military force and, failing that, at least sought a clear enforcement mechanism. Wilson was aware that this would be politically unacceptable in America. Article 10 was a compromise which left it open to the League to decide at the time how each crisis should best be handled. Even the vague commitment implicit in Article 10 worried many, and the Americans were not alone in their concerns. At the very first meeting of the League, in 1920, Canada unsuccessfully tried to have it suppressed. It made another attempt in 1922 to have it agreed that no member could be obliged to go to war without the consent of its parliament or legislature. In 1923, Canada was central to another debate arguing that Article 10 obligations should be interpreted as an optional rather than a binding commitment. Although these efforts did not succeed they enjoyed significant support. Two schools of thought were evolving as to the role of the League. One, supported by France, saw the League as a vehicle for collective security, the other, which included Britain and its dominions, saw the League as facilitating discussion. With such a divergence it was increasingly unlikely that the League would provide an instrument for ensuring its members against aggression, as would be borne out by events in the 1930s.

The issue of America's rejection of membership in the League of Nations was controversial and deeply divisive in the United States. Later one of Wilson's disciples, Franklin Roosevelt, would engineer American entry into the League's successor, the United Nations. America's absence probably did weaken the League, but the controversy over Article 10 should be seen in a wider context as part of an ongoing debate about how, if at all possible, to arrange for collective security.

ORGANIZATION

The Covenant's preamble set out the objectives of the organization [*Doc. 8*]. The business of the League was divided between three bodies: the Assembly, the Council, and the Secretariat. The Assembly was comprised of up to three representatives from each member state, though each state could cast only one vote. In normal circumstances the Assembly was to meet annually, usually convening in September. It could only discuss issues and make recommendations to the Council, but it controlled the budget, the admission of new members by a two-thirds vote, and the election of non-permanent members to the Council. The League began with forty-two members and by 1925 had grown to fifty-four.

The Council was originally intended to consist of nine members, five permanent and four non-permanent. The original permanent member states were Britain, France, Italy, Japan, and the United States, but with the American rejection its seat was never occupied. In 1925, in the aftermath of the Locarno Pact, Germany was admitted as a permanent member. Later in the League's turbulent history Germany and Italy would resign their memberships, while the Soviet Union was a permanent member during 1934–39. Non-permanent seats were increased to six in 1922 and nine in 1926, with members elected every three years. The Council normally met every four months, but in times of crisis would convene more frequently. In a conflict any member state could bring its grievance before the Council. If a state refused to accept the decision of the Council and continued aggressive activity, the Council's one weapon was to have other members apply economic and financial sanctions against the aggressor. The Council did have the power to recommend military action, but never did so.

A secretary-general appointed by the Council and approved by the Assembly led the Secretariat. The Secretariat saw to the vast amount of clerical work required by the League. The first secretary-general was Eric Drummond, a British diplomat, who served in that post from 1919 to 1933 and who did much to establish the League as a functional organization.

In terms of innovation the Assembly was a milestone in the development of international relations, a body with a worldwide membership convened not to discuss a particular issue but which held a remit over the entire field of international relations. Here both great and small powers spoke with equality. The Council was, in some ways, an institutionalization of the old Concert system, which had been dominated by the Great Powers, in this instance the permanent members being the great powers. From the beginning it was hoped the United States would take its seat and it was assumed that, in due course, Germany and Russia would as well. Originally it was intended that the Great Powers would enjoy a majority though this never occurred.

The League commenced work in 1920, the headquarters being established at Geneva, in neutral Switzerland. Functioning under the control of the League were several subsidiary political bodies, including the Permanent Commission on Mandates, the High Commission for Danzig, and the Commission overseeing France's occupation of the Saar. There were also a range of technical bodies, the most notable being the Committee on Intellectual Cooperation, the Advisory Committee on Traffic in Opium and Dangerous Drugs, and the Refugee Organization. Finally there were a number of organizations that operated autonomously but which were dependent on the League, including the International Labour Organization and the Permanent Court of International Justice.

The Permanent Court of International Justice (PCIJ), often referred to as the World Court, located at The Hague in the Netherlands was one of the major innovations of the League. The establishment of this body was the culmination of many centuries of development in international law. Since the sixteenth century there had been increasing discussion of how to apply the rule of law to international relations. The nineteenth century had witnessed the development of treaties by which states agreed to seek arbitration of disputes, and at the 1899 First Hague Conference an International Court of Arbitration was established at The Hague, a body that still exists. The 1907 Second Hague Conference sought to go further, calling for the establishment of a permanent court to settle inter-state judicial issues, but no agreement about its composition was reached before the outbreak of war in 1914. The Covenant provided for such a court, the PCIJ, which was formally opened in December 1922, also at The Hague. States, not individuals, would be the parties before the court, and its services were available to all League members as well as any other states which agreed to accept the jurisdiction of the court and to carry out its decisions. The court was empowered to hear cases concerning interpretation of treaties, questions of international law, the existence of any fact that if established would constitute a breach of international obligation, and the nature of reparation to be made for any such breach. Although the United States never joined the League, nor adhered to the court, many prominent American jurists served on its bench.

The peace treaties provided for the former overseas colonies of Germany and the Middle East portions of the Ottoman Empire to be placed under the League of Nations, with their administration being provided by various members of the League. The Covenant set out that these territories were to be governed with the interests and progress of the inhabitants as the primary objective. The mandates were classified as 'A', 'B', and 'C'. The 'A' mandates, which were all formerly part of the Ottoman Empire, covered countries whose inhabitants were considered almost ready to run their own affairs. 'B' mandates, comprising most of Germany's former possessions in Africa and the Pacific, were those where it was decided that the inhabitants were not yet prepared to administer their own government; while the 'C' mandates, made up from the remainder of Germany's Pacific colonies, were seen as sufficiently under-developed as to be best administered by the mandatory power as if it were an integral part of its own territory. The mandates system was one of the significant innovations of the League. There were some precedents; for example, the Ionian Islands had been administered in this way by Britain (1815–64) and Morocco, by France after the 1906 Algeciras Conference. The League institutionalized the concept, providing a mechanism for oversight.

The concept behind the mandates system was that these territories were not the spoils of war, but the responsibility of developed states that had entered under formal obligation to govern them in the best interests of the inhabitants with the ultimate intention of preparing them for independence. To ensure that these obligations were being carried out the League established a Permanent Mandates Commission to receive and comment upon the annual reports of the mandatory powers and, in turn, to pass their observations on to the Council of the League. The system was not without its difficulties. Most of the mandates were assigned to states that were also permanent members of the Council. These states, in practice, wished for minimum interference in their administration of their mandates and, using the Council, they successfully blocked members of the permanent Mandates Commission from visiting these territories for inspections. As a result, information was limited to an annual report provided by the mandatory power to the League. Although the Commission had no power to remove a mandatory state or give it instruction, the mere fact of oversight and the obligation to report was a significant step in the growth of international governance.

The International Labour Organization (ILO) was the outcome of the great demands placed on workers during the war which, in turn, caused their leaders to desire a voice in the postwar order. The Russian Revolution had also increased the demands of workers internationally, even if they did not support Marxist ideology. While the Paris Peace Conference was meeting, a labour union congress was held simultaneously at Berne, Switzerland which called for an international labour parliament. The peacemakers were, therefore, anxious to find a way to provide a voice in international affairs for workers and it responded by setting up a special commission on international labour legislation headed by the American labour leader, Samuel Gompers. Its recommendations led to the creation of the ILO under the League of Nations. The ILO embodied a compromise between the highest expectations of the labour movement and the concerns of government and industry. It was hoped that the ILO would reduce the threat of war by improving labour conditions and living standards through economic and social stability, with its constitution stating its aim as the promotion of 'Lasting Peace Through Social Justice'.

The ILO was provided with an innovative structure for an international organization. The organization comprised three parts, an annual conference, a governing body for coordinating policy, and an International Labour Office. The secretariat collected information on such subjects as child labour and working hours that formed the basis for the ILO's members adopting conventions setting minimum standards. The conference was to meet annually. The member states sent four delegates each, two representing the government, and one each representing employers and workers respectively to the annual conference. Delegates did not have to vote as a state unit and, therefore, it was possible for employers' representatives or labour representatives to vote across state lines. For the first time at an official, international level interest groups were being provided with an independent voice.

The ILO's first meeting was held at Washington, DC, in October 1919 (before the United States rejected membership of the League of Nations), and chose as its first director-general the moderate French Socialist politician Albert Thomas. Despite the setback of American rejection the ILO enjoyed a more universal appeal than even the League, admitting Germany and Austria in 1919. This universality and the effective work of the ILO even led the United States, which otherwise shunned the League, to join the ILO under a special arrangement in 1934.

The Committee on Intellectual Cooperation was another organ of the League, intended to improve the condition of intellectual workers and to promote international contacts. This body looked at ways to protect copyright, promote academic exchanges and provide a clearinghouse for information. It initially suffered from lack of funds until 1924, when the French government offered to establish at Paris an International Institute of

Intellectual Cooperation, working under the committee. The members of the committee were a notable assemblage and included such figures as Albert Einstein and Marie Curie. After the Second World War its work was continued by UNESCO.

THE WORK OF THE LEAGUE

At first many states were sceptical that the League would play a significant role in international relations, particularly after its rejection by the United States. Its utility, though, soon became apparent, solving at least low-level problems and providing a forum in which diplomats and statesmen could meet. Its growing importance can be seen in the first visit by a British prime minister in 1924, and the practice adopted from 1925 by many states of being represented by their foreign minister. Not only did the League and Open Diplomacy flourish, but the meetings in Geneva also provided an opportunity for some quiet and less visible diplomacy.

In the early years of the League its opportunity to resolve major inter-national issues was overshadowed by the continuing existence of the wartime Allied Supreme Council, in the form of the Conference of Ambassadors, which continued to exist until 1924 at Paris. It took the lead in resolving such crises as the Corfu incident of 1923 between Greece and Italy. While the League did not play the primary role in settling the Corfu incident it did assist by applying pressure upon Italy. Only after the 1925 Locarno Pact, and the winding up of the Conference of Ambassadors, did the League Council emerge as the primary international forum. The Great Powers, however, did turn to the League after they had failed to resolve two important crises and, in turn, the League was successful. These accomplishments were settling the German-Polish frontier in Upper Silesia and saving Austria (and later Hungary, Bulgaria and Greece) from financial crises.

The first crisis brought directly before the League was the future of the Åland Islands. These islands had historically formed part of Finland but their population was largely Swedish. Under a treaty of 1856 the islands were permanently demilitarized. The status of the islands arose again when Finland became independent, as a consequence of the Russian revolution, and the Åland islanders, claiming the right of self-determination, demanded annexation to Sweden. The Finnish government granted the islands autonomy in May 1920, but separatist agitation continued and, in June, the secessionist leaders were arrested and charged with treason. This brought about Finno-Swedish tension and later that same month the matter was brought before the League Council. With the consent of the disputants a League commission of jurists was established which recommended, after investigation, that the islands remain within Finland, with a special status and that a new neutralization and demilitarization convention be agreed.

This was accepted by Finland and Sweden and came into effect in 1922, providing the League with its first significant success at resolving international tension.

The League also was responsible for the first bail out of a faltering national economy by an international organization, foreshadowing work that would become the responsibility of the International Monetary Fund after the Second World War. The first country to face financial catastrophe in which the League intervened was Austria. As a result of the war, it no longer lay at the hub of a great empire and its economic life lay in ruins. In 1921, the League had made an abortive attempt to reschedule Austria's debt and impose strict restructuring of the country's finances, but this had foundered on the ambivalent attitude of Washington to a plan initiated by the League of Nations. By 1922, though, Austria was on the verge of collapse, an event that would threaten the fragile stability of central Europe. The League responded by proposing a financial restructuring package with the key powers guaranteeing a $120 million loan aimed at stabilizing the Austrian economy. The League would have oversight in order to see that reforms were implemented and the loans repaid. The mere announcement of the plan did much to calm the situation, confidence was slowly restored and by 1925 the special League oversight was ended. The League here played a role that no single state could have accomplished.

The League also played a central role in alleviating the refugee crisis spawned by the war. There were not only the refugees brought about by the First World War, but also those caused by the Russian revolution and, then in the wake of the Greco-Turkish war (1921–22), the exodus of over one million ethnic Greeks from Turkey. In 1921 it established the Refugee Organization with Fritjof Nansen as its High Commissioner. Among the many problems the refugees faced was the absence of valid documents that would allow them to cross borders in a return home. The League resolved this by issuing 'Nansen passports' which would enable the refugees to travel across borders. Originally meant as a temporary organization to assist displaced persons, the Refugee Organization became a permanent part of the League's work. Nansen was awarded the 1922 Nobel Peace Prize for his work.

As the League Council came to enjoy enhanced prominence, so its success at fostering cooperation encouraged some to see it as a model for other future developments. In a proposal that, in retrospect, has assumed great importance the French premier, Edouard Herriot, stated in 1925 that he saw in the League of Nations a rough draft for a scheme for a United States of Europe. In 1929 his successor Aristide Briand proposed a scheme for a European Union. The ideas being debated in the years immediately following the First World War provided some of the earliest development of the scheme for the creation of a European Union, based in part on the experience gained from the League of Nations.

CONCLUSION

The reputation of the League has suffered in retrospect from its inability to deter the aggressor states in the 1930s. Some argue that the League, while conceptually sound, ultimately failed because of the times in which it existed and unfortunate circumstances. Failure is variously attributed to the unanticipated rise of aggressor states in the 1930s, the failure of the United States to join, the initial exclusion of Germany and Soviet Russia, the embodying of the Covenant in the peace treaties, thereby associating it with the victors and, as a consequence, preventing it from the start being an organization open to all states. A wider argument is also made that the initial objectives of the League were too ambitious for the international system as it existed and that the League, as a result, could not possibly have been made a more robust structure. In a world of sovereign states, committing in advance to be bound by the decisions of a mutual organization has always proven difficult. It was politically unrealistic to expect that the authors of the Covenant would have accepted any greater derogation of authority to this new creature in international relations. F.H. Hinsley, one of the leading writers on the history of international relations, argued of the League's primary objective of maintaining peace that, 'it is impossible to organise the world on such a principle for very long. However logical and impressive it may seem in theory, it cannot stand the strain of peace-time relationships.'[2]

The ultimate failure of the League should not be allowed to overshadow its substantive achievements. During the first two years of its existence the League, for example, resolved the Åland Islands dispute between Finland and Sweden, oversaw the repatriation of just under half a million prisoners of war from twenty-six countries, launched a campaign against typhus, and initiated the process of establishing general codes for railways, ports, and waterways. Particularly notable was the appointment of Nansen as High Commissioner for Refugees to deal with the some one and a half million refugees and displaced persons that were one of the results of the war.

Notes

1 'publicists': writers on or persons skilled in international law (*jus publicum* public law).
2 F.H. Hinsley, *Power and the Pursuit of Peace* (Cambridge, 1963), p. 321.

CHAPTER FIVE

SOVIET RUSSIA

In 1917, Lenin and the Bolshevik communists successfully seized power in the Russian capital and rapidly extended their control over many areas of the country. It was to take until 1921 before they were firmly in control of the entire country. The forces of the 'Red' communists now became embroiled in a civil war with the anti-communist 'White' forces. Lenin removed Russia from the war, leading to an Allied military intervention intended both to protect the military supplies they had already provided Russia, but also to support the effort of those White Russian leaders who might bring Russia back into the war. The first act of Lenin's regime was the Decree on Peace, issued the day after the revolution, which called for a just and democratic peace, a peace without annexations or indemnities, a peace on the basis of self-determination, and the end of secret diplomacy. In many ways this was much more characteristic of Wilson than Marx. While it seemed even-handed, it was actually anti-Allied. At the time the Central Powers' policy called for no annexations as they planned, instead, on the establishment of puppet states. The Allied powers did plan annexations; for example, France's ambitions to re-annex Alsace–Lorraine, Italy's hopes of seizing the South Tyrol, and the whole web of secret treaties for the division of the Ottoman Empire. When the Bolsheviks took over the foreign ministry at Petrograd they found in the archives copies of the secret treaties and took great glee in publishing them. This action had a great impact and would lead some to argue that the war was no more than an act of Anglo-French expansionism. In this light Lenin's call for no annexations can be seen as a strongly anti-western act.

Lenin was also acting for domestic reasons. Many people expected that the new government would end the war, hopefully without the loss of territory. Lenin was aware, however, that some territory would have to be lost to Russia. It was one reason why he called for a peace without annexations, instead of referring to loss of land, as he knew that the Central Powers intended to create a series of puppet states for example, in Poland,

Estonia, Latvia, and Lithuania. In diplomacy actions can be divided between declaratory and operational. The Decree on Peace was Lenin's first declaratory action in foreign policy. A few days later he took his first operational act when he contacted the German High Command for an armistice. The Germans were delighted, they already held what territory they desired and this would allow them to shift forces to the western front.

Peace negotiations were held at Brest-Litovsk, with Trotsky as the chief Russian negotiator. Shocked by the German demands Trotsky broke off the negotiations. Lenin was now faced by demands from some of his followers, such as Bukharin, for a revolutionary war of defence. Lenin, however, was determined upon peace and convinced Trotsky to return to the negotiations. Trotsky tried a new formula of 'no peace, no war'. While prolonging the armistice, and thus avoiding any resumption of the fighting, he hoped to propagandize the German soldiers to support the communist cause, even showering the German lines with propaganda by balloon.

The German government responded by ordering the army to resume hostilities. It also concluded a treaty with the separatist Ukrainian government. All this put more pressure on the Bolsheviks to agree to a peace and it helped to convince some of Lenin's more dubious followers of the necessity of signing a peace treaty, regardless of its severity. By the Treaty of Brest-Litovsk in March 1918 Russia lost one-third of its population including Finland, the Baltic Provinces, Poland, the Ukraine, and territory in the Caucasus. The treaty also gives some sense of the terms Germany would have imposed on the western powers if it had ultimately won the war. Later, when Germany was defeated by the Allies, Lenin abrogated the Brest-Litovsk agreement. Having made peace, Lenin now faced Allied military intervention.

THE INTERVENTION AND THE CIVIL WAR

The Allied intervention was not driven by fear of ideological danger or as part of a crusade against communism; at the time they had other concerns. The Allies presumed that Lenin was in league with Germany. After all, it was Germany that had facilitated Lenin's return to Russia from Switzerland in 1917. His willingness to make peace with Germany, on Germany's terms, and the establishment of diplomatic relations, seemed to confirm this. The degree of Lenin's complicity with Germany remains an open question. Russia's withdrawal from the war was a major setback to the Allies and at the very least they were anxious to secure the substantial supplies they had already provided to Russia. It was also in their interest to support any group that might continue the war effort. Several potential leaders had emerged and organized armies to counter the Bolsheviks and by the summer of 1918 there were eighteen anti-Bolshevik governments scattered across

Russia. Prominent among these was one led by General Denikin whose army was in control of parts of Southern Russia, while in Siberia there was another group under Admiral Kolchak. Kolchak had established his headquarters at Omsk and soon emerged as preeminent among the White cause. The Omsk government was represented at the Paris Peace Conference by Sazonov, who had once been foreign minister in the old tsarist regime. These various anti-Bolshevik leaders never truly tried to meet the interests of the Allies or of the many oppressed nationalities. In general they sought to re-establish the old Russian empire and, as a result, were reluctant to recognize any territorial losses. Kolchak, for example, refused to give the Allies assurances that he accepted the independence of Finland and the three Baltic states. Denikin likewise was extremely anti-Polish and sought to suppress any Ukrainian independence movement. At the fringes of the old Russian state there were many separatist movements. In January 1918 Ukraine had proclaimed its independence and this was acknowledged in the Brest-Litovsk treaty. This was followed by the peoples of the Caucasus, with Armenia, Azerbaijan, and Georgia all proclaiming their independence. The situation became enormously complex, with several groups at times claiming authority over the same area.

Planning for an intervention began immediately after Lenin's seizure of power with the first phase of the intervention stretching from the summer of 1918 to November 1918. For the Allies this was seen as part of their war against the Central Powers. Northern Russia, around the important ports of Archangel and Murmansk, was occupied by a force provided by Britain, which already had some forces at Murmansk from an earlier deployment, France, the United States, and Serbia. The British also despatched a force to the Caucasus, where it already had substantial oil interests. The French, meanwhile, occupied the key Ukrainian port of Odessa. Japan had been eager to occupy the area around Vladivostok, but the Americans opposed this fearing that Japan was seeking territorial gain. Wilson finally agreed to a joint Allied landing there, largely to help evacuate the Czech Legion. Japan eventually had 75,000 troops in the area and its reluctance to withdraw was one of the causes of American-Japanese tension after the war. Greece and Italy also provided troops.

A particularly complicated situation arose surrounding the Czech Legion. This force had been formed from Czech soldiers who had been serving in the Austro-Hungarian army, had been captured by the Russians, and who had then been organized into a force to fight for the Allies with the object of seeing the creation of an independent Czech state. This force had been in the process of being transported via Siberia to the port of Vladivostok, from which they would travel by ship to western Europe. They would be a valuable asset to the war-weary troops on the western front, but under the terms of the Brest-Litovsk treaty Germany had insisted

they be disarmed. Seeing that they might be trapped in Russia the Czechs revolted and in so doing became an independent military force that sought to fight its way out of Russia, making its way along the trans-Siberian railway towards Vladivostok. Numbering about 50,000 soldiers they placed their military power at the service of local leaders or groups who could facilitate their passage. At one stage, in August 1918, it even looked as if they might take Moscow itself. It was at this point that Trotsky embarked on his organization of a new, Red Army. It was the effectiveness of this force in the fighting that ensured the communist victory.

With the end of the war in November the intervention entered a new phase, with the foreign forces in Russia openly engaging in anti-Bolshevik activities. There was no need to fear a prostrate Soviet Russia. The concern lay with the potential for social unrest in their own countries given the example set by the Bolsheviks and possibly aided by them. These efforts, however, were plagued by poor coordination. For example, both Britain and France offered support to General Denikin, leader of one of the White Russian armies, while at the same time they were supporting nationalist movements in Ukraine and the Caucasus that Denikin opposed. The Allied intervention proved to be a half-hearted event. With the end of the war the primary reason for intervention had disappeared. The soldiers despatched to Russia, for the most part, were either exhausted from the war or of poor quality. The bewildering political landscape of revolutionary Russia was hard to navigate and, just as the Allies found it difficult to cooperate so, too, did the opposition to Lenin. By the summer of 1919 the Allies had had enough and began to evacuate their forces. All that remained by the end of the year was a British force at Batum that stayed until 1921 and the Japanese in eastern Siberia. The last foreign forces left Russia in 1925 when the Japanese withdrew from the northern part of Sakhalin island.

Various national breakaway states had taken the opportunity to attempt to establish their independence amid the chaos of the Russian revolution. Finland had declared independence, citing a promise by Lenin some months earlier to liberate the country. Lenin reluctantly agreed. The political struggle occurring in Russia would now also be played out in Finland, with a civil war between communist and non-communist forces. Moscow was not in a position to provide much aid to the Finnish communists and the result was that Russia would be bordered by a non-communist Finland. The Baltic provinces of Estonia, Latvia, and Lithuania had all been occupied by German forces during the war. As the Germans withdrew Soviet forces and local communists were able, in most areas, to defeat nationalists seeking to establish independent republics. Throughout 1919, however, the nationalists aided by Finland and some German army units were able to turn the tide. During 1920, a series of peace treaties was concluded between these states and Moscow, recognizing their independence.

Other independence movements were less successful. In the Caucasus a number of conflicting governments and administrations had been established. After the Russian revolution a shortlived Transcaucasian federation was established, but this had broken down by early 1918 and been replaced by independent republics in Armenia, Azerbaijan, and Georgia, none of which were supportive of the Bolshevik regime in Moscow. The Armenian state had hoped that its future would be assured by the Treaty of Sèvres, which envisaged an independent Armenia. President Wilson was asked to determine its frontiers, and his proposal would have created a great state stretching from the Caucasus and the Black Sea to the Mediterranean. Neither the Bolsheviks nor the Turkish nationalists had anything to gain from such a state, and this helped bring about a Soviet-Turkish friendship treaty. Turkish nationalist forces invaded Armenia and, in desperation, the Armenian government was forced to turn to Moscow. Soviet forces occupied Armenia and absorbed it into the Soviet state in November 1920. As a result historic Armenia lay divided between Soviet Russia and Turkey along its prewar borders, though now with the vast majority of Armenians living in Soviet Armenia after the wartime depopulation of the Armenian portions of the Ottoman Empire. Most of the Armenians remaining in Turkey fled to Lebanon and Syria.

In Azerbaijan an independent republic had been created in early 1918 with Turkish and, subsequently, British support, the latter having intervened to protect the oilfields. British forces withdrew in August 1919 and in May 1920 the Soviet army occupied the territory. Georgia was unusual in being dominated, after the collapse of the Transcaucasian federation, by the Menshevik branch of Russian marxism. The Mensheviks proclaimed an independent Georgian republic in May 1918 which was recognized by Moscow in May 1920. This, however, did not prevent Soviet forces from invading Georgia once it was strong enough to do so, in early 1921. Loss of its independence would lead to a rebellion in 1924 that was brutally suppressed. In Ukraine an independent government had been established during the war and recognized by the Central Powers, which it supported. Ukraine too was caught up in the revolutionary fervour of the period and Bolshevik forces vied with national forces.

THE RUSSO-POLISH WAR

Poland had disappeared as an independent state during the eighteenth century when it was partitioned by Russia, Prussia, and Austria. With the collapse of these empires at the end of the First World War Poland reemerged as an independent state. The Paris Peace Conference proposed as the new country's eastern frontier a line, known as the Curzon Line, which included within Poland all those districts of a definitely Polish character. The Polish government, however, claimed a frontier much further east on historical grounds. The German evacuation of the contested district combined with Russia's distraction in a civil war provided an opportunity for Poland to implement its claims and it established its forces further to the east. The Bolsheviks also attempted to occupy the evacuated districts. The Poles were concerned that the Russian forces would in due course turn against Poland. Lenin hoped that the Russian revolution would ignite a world revolution and, in particular, there was great hope of revolution in Germany. For Lenin and his followers the bridge to Europe lay through Poland. The defeat of the right-wing Kapp putsch in Germany in March 1920 by a general strike led Lenin to believe the time was ripe for a revolution in Germany.

The Polish leader, Pilsudski, decided upon a preemptive strike in April 1920. The war at first went well for the Poles who invaded Ukraine and took Kiev in early May. The Poles had hoped to install a friendly government, but it enjoyed little domestic support. In June the Red Army counter-attacked and drove the Polish army back to the outskirts of Warsaw. In the Battle of Warsaw, during August 1920, the westward advance of the Red army was checked, the Poles took 100,000 prisoners and again began to advance. The war also saw the last great cavalry charges in European warfare. An armistice was agreed to in October. By the Treaty of Riga in March 1921 Poland received a frontier substantially to the east of the Curzon Line. Poland had also taken the opportunity, in October 1920, to seize the city of Vilna. Lithuania also claimed this city and had established its capital there. This crisis soured Polish-Lithuanian relations between the two World Wars, preventing any security cooperation. The Red Army now turned its attention to the residual White Armies and by the end of 1921 the White cause had been defeated. The Russian Civil War and the Russo-Polish War, running between 1918 and 1922, caused more casualties than the European conflict of 1914–18. In Russia alone 12.5 million people died.

THE QUEST FOR RECOGNITION

It is not uncommon for revolutionary regimes to reject the normal modes of diplomatic conduct, claiming instead the correctness of their new way of doing things. Eventually, the need to conduct business with other states led these revolutionary states slowly to adopt the traditional methods of diplomatic relations. Immediately after the revolution Trotsky, as the newly appointed commissar for foreign affairs, proclaimed that 'All there is to do is to publish the secret treaties. Then I will close the shop.'[1] Later as the Soviet regime needed to conduct business with other states it sought normal diplomatic relations. No state had as yet extended *de jure* recognition to Lenin's regime, and much of the diplomatic activity of the early period of the Soviet government was a quest for diplomatic recognition.

Trotsky was soon moved to military matters and was replaced by

Chicherin who, while a committed communist, tended to follow the classical tradition in diplomacy and sought equal relations with both sides engaged in the war. The first governments to accord Soviet Russia normal diplomatic relations were the three Baltic republics of Estonia, Latvia, and Lithuania. This provided Russia with a valuable channel for commercial relations with the rest of the world which Lenin urgently sought in order to assist the task of reconstruction. The impact of first the war and then the civil war had disrupted agricultural production, causing a great famine during 1921–22. Humanitarian assistance was provided by the United States through the American Relief Organization headed by Herbert Hoover. This led to hopes that the United States would open relations, but American interest went no further than humanitarian concerns and the United States did not recognize the communist government until 1933. The reluctance of the western states to recognize the Soviet government was not just ideological but also financial. On taking power Lenin's regime had repudiated Russia's substantial foreign debt. Since the 1880s Russia had been engaged in a massive effort at industrialization, heavily financed by foreign capital in particular from France and Belgium. To these debts can be added the great wartime loans from their allies.

Shunned by the western powers, the only option for Soviet Russia was to turn to Europe's other pariah state, Germany. With the Brest-Litovsk treaty Germany had recognized the Bolshevik regime, but with the defeat of Germany the new government there did not renew relations with Moscow. By 1921, out of necessity, this had begun to change as Germany was also ostracized by the Allied powers. Commercial relations were beginning, while quite separately the German army was developing its own relations with the communist regime. This provided the background for the resumption of full diplomatic relations.

In 1922 the Allies convened a conference at Genoa to discuss European economic reconstruction. Germany and Soviet Russia were also invited to attend, as a practical matter. The Russian delegation travelled via Berlin, providing the opportunity for further negotiations. The Genoa Conference ultimately achieved very little and, during most of it, the Germans and Russians were shunned except when there was some special need to involve them. The great surprise of the conference came while the Allies were celebrating Easter, when the Russians and Germans concluded a treaty in the neigbouring town of Rapallo. The Treaty of Rapallo re-established diplomatic relations and both sides renounced any past financial claims against the other. This led soon after to secret military collaboration that allowed Germany to build factories in Russia to produce weapons forbidden by the Versailles treaty. In return, the Soviet government benefited from the development of its armaments industry and technical training. This secret relationship would last for a decade.

Among the major western leaders only Lloyd George showed interest in opening relations with Moscow though he faced opposition from some of his cabinet colleagues, especially Churchill and the foreign secretary, Lord Curzon [*Doc. 5*]. As it became clear that the anti-Bolshevik forces were unlikely to succeed Lloyd George had begun to withdraw British forces from Russia. Britain's postwar economic slump led Lloyd George to consider the possibilities available in opening the vast Russian market and in 1921 an Anglo-Soviet trade agreement was reached according *de facto*, if not *de jure*, recognition. Relations were less friendly during the Conservative government that succeeded Lloyd George at the end of 1922, but improved again when Ramsay Macdonald formed Britain's first Labour government in 1924. Macdonald took the lead in extending *de jure* recognition, an action followed by the end of the year by Italy, France and several other European states.

THE COMINTERN

In the conduct of foreign affairs the Soviet government made use not only of its foreign ministry but also an organization known as the Comintern (Communist International). In effect, the Soviet regime was conducting a two-level foreign policy. Through its foreign ministry it was seeking normal diplomatic relations while through the Comintern it sought to promote its vision of a world revolution. The Comintern was a useful mechanism that allowed the Soviet government to claim that it was not promoting the overthrow of governments with which it sought diplomatic relations. The Soviet government always maintained the fiction that the Comintern was no more than a private organization that just happened to be located in Moscow. In reality, though, the Comintern was another arm of the Soviet regime. Led by one of Lenin's closest colleagues, Zinoviev, it held its first congress in Moscow in 1919. Of the thirty-four delegates, thirty were employed by the foreign ministry, two were visitors to Moscow who were invited to attend, and only two were delegates sent by other communist parties. The hope had been to take advantage of what seemed to be the rising tide of revolutionary fervour during 1919. By 1920 this had subsided and at the second congress of the Comintern, held that year, the focus was on the criteria for membership. The 'Twenty-One Conditions' were designed to ensure that communist parties were under the control of Moscow and not acting independently. These conditions required parties to break with any labour group that would not adhere to the leadership of Moscow. In most countries this led to a split in the socialist movement and the establishment of small parties firmly under the control of Moscow. These communist parties usually did not attract established leaders and their members were not well known. As a result, their prestige depended upon being recognized by the Comintern and this kept them loyal to Moscow's policies. A similar split occurred when the communists began attempting to establish their position in the trades union movement, usually leading to the creation of separate communist-led unions. During this first phase the Comintern may have acted at times without coordination with the foreign ministry, though Stalin would later see to it that it was firmly under central control.

Zinoviev, an advocate of pursuing world revolution, embarked on a series of unsuccessful efforts to spur revolution in other countries. Having failed in Europe during 1919, attention turned to Central Asia where a Congress of Peoples of the East was held in Baku in 1920, where efforts were made to promote the communist cause in Afghanistan, Iran, and Turkey, though with little success. Greater progress was made in China where a communist party was founded in 1920. Initially it was very successful in building its position in cooperation with the Kuomingtang (Nationalist) party. Sun Yat-sen (Sun Yixian) founded the party in 1911 and he was succeeded, in 1925, by Chiang Kai-shek (Jiang Jieshi). Fearing that the communists might take over the Kuomingtang, Chiang Kai-shek moved against them in 1926, and more fully in 1927, almost destroying the communist party. There was also some early communist success in the Dutch East Indies (Indonesia), but an attempted communist uprising was crushed in 1926. These failures contributed to Zinoviev being replaced in 1926.

The chief target of the Comintern was Britain, which was viewed as Soviet Russia's prime adversary. In the assessment of the communist leadership the one state that could cause the greatest threat was Britain. This led the Comintern to support independence movements in Britain's empire as a way both to distract and ultimately weaken this potential adversary. This illustrates the reality that the Comintern was intended to serve the interests of Soviet Russia. When Afghanistan fought a brief war with Britain in 1919 and, in effect, established its independence of Britain, the Soviet government hastened to extend diplomatic relations and to praise a feudal, monarchical regime. At the 1920 Baku congress the participants were exhorted to wage a holy war against British imperialism. The lack of coordination between the Comintern and other aspects of Soviet foreign policy could cause occasional setbacks. While waging an active campaign against Britain on one front, on another the Soviet government was attempting to establish working trade and diplomatic relations with London.

In October 1924 Britain's first Labour government, led by Ramsay MacDonald, lost a vote of confidence in the House of Commons which necessitated a general election. The next day the Foreign Office was sent a copy of a letter, supposedly from Zinoviev addressed to the central committee of the Communist Party of Great Britain. It urged the party to stir up the British working class in preparation for class war. Later that month the letter was leaked to a national newspaper, the *Daily Mail*, igniting a political furore. It was a major embarrassment for MacDonald, who had recognized the Soviet government. Four days later Labour was defeated by the Conservatives.

The authenticity of the 'Zinoviev Letter', and how it came to appear in the press at such a critical moment, remained a source of debate. In 1999 the British government commissioned a study to determine what actually occurred, with full access to all records and with the cooperation of Moscow. It determined that the letter was indeed a forgery, but that the Foreign Office thought it was genuine. No evidence was found that the British intelligence service was responsible but it is likely that two of its officers were involved in leaking it to the press and to the Conservative party.

CONCLUSION

In May 1922 Lenin suffered the first of a series of strokes which led to his death in 1924. During this period the main energies of the political leadership were engaged in a struggle for Lenin's mantle. As Stalin emerged as the leader in the years after Lenin's death the confusions and lack of coordination of Soviet foreign policy ceased. However, the regime Lenin established in 1917 altered many of the precepts of the international system and introduced an ideological dimension which would increasingly pit the revolutionary Marxism of Lenin against the liberal democratic ideals of the United States. There was concern that Lenin's pronouncements would appeal to many people in a war-ravaged and exhausted Europe. Wilson's speech of the Fourteen Points, given not long after Lenin's seizure of power, was not only meant to provide a framework for a peace settlement, but also to provide an alternative to Lenin's rhetoric. After the end of the war Europe could be divided into three groups of states, the victors, the vanquished, and Russia. Among the victors Russia was seen not as a factor causing stability but rather as the major threat to stability. The 1922 German-Soviet rapprochement was therefore a matter of great concern and would provide a central motivation in the moves that soon ensued to rehabilitate Germany and thereby split it from Russia. In many ways the road to Locarno began at Rapallo.

Note

1   Quoted in *The Proletarian Revolution* (Moscow) 10 (Oct. 1922), p. 99.

CHAPTER SIX

THE EASTERN MEDITERRANEAN

The postwar situation in the eastern Mediterranean was dominated by the consequences of the collapse of the Ottoman Empire. For over a century the Eastern Question, which concerned the fate of the Ottoman Empire, had been a major problem in international relations and an area of tension between the Great Powers. British forces played a significant role in the defeat of the Ottoman Empire and by 1918 had seized control of an area stretching from the Mediterranean to the borders of Iran. In October 1918 the Ottoman government asked for an armistice and Britain, excluding the French from the negotiations, concluded one off Mudros, aboard HMS *Agamemnon*. The exclusion of France was indicative of the long-running competition between Britain and France for hegemony in the eastern Mediterranean. While they were global allies in the conduct of the war, they were longstanding regional rivals. Allied forces entered Constantinople and surrounding areas and Sultan Mehmed VI became virtually a prisoner of the Allies. The British navy now controlled the Dardanelles, the French had occupied Adana and the region of Cilicia, while the Italians had occupied the area around Antalya (Adalia), the chief port of southern Anatolia. The Ottoman Empire's fate was already the subject of numerous wartime secret treaties, agreements, and declarations. Several of these were contradictory and would provide the source for much postwar inter-Allied tension.

THE SECRET TREATIES

During the war the Allies had concluded among themselves a series of secret agreements dealing with the future of the Ottoman Empire, reached either to induce states to enter the conflict on the Allied side, or to prevent disagreements among the Allies as to the eventual disposal of the potential spoils of war. Wartime events had led to some adaptation of these agreements. All these agreements presumed the end of the Ottoman Empire, although a small, rump state might be left in part of Anatolia.

It had originally been agreed, in the 1915 Constantinople Agreement between Britain, France, and Russia, that the last would be given Constantinople and the Straits. Russia's withdrawal caused the promise of Constantinople to lapse, and the remaining key allies could not agree a replacement. It was also agreed in 1915, in the Treaty of London, that Italy would receive outright ownership of the Dodecanese islands, which it had seized in 1911. It was also promised, in vague terms, a share of the Ottoman Empire adjacent to Antalya. In April 1916 Britain, Russia, and France agreed that in the Middle East Britain would have a sphere of influence over Mesopotamia (Iraq) and the Mediterranean ports of Acre and Haifa, France would have a sphere of influence over Adana, Cilicia, southern Kurdistan and part of the Syrian coast, Russia would receive the part of Armenia under Ottoman rule and part of Kurdistan, and Palestine would be internationalized. In 1917, in the Treaty of Saint-Jean de Maurienne, Britain, France, and Italy agreed that France would receive control of the Adana region and Italy would receive more territory up the coast from Antalya, opposite the Dodecanese islands. During 1916 an Anglo-French agreement, known as the Sykes–Picot agreement after the negotiators, made more specific the 1916 agreement's provisions concerning the Middle East and gave Britain a sphere of influence over Mesopotamia and Palestine; France a sphere over Syria, Adana, Cilicia, and southern Kurdistan, and Russia was given an additional zone of influence over Armenia, part of Kurdistan, and parts of northeastern Anatolia.

The British government had also been in correspondence during the war with the Emir Hussein of Mecca, hoping to bring about an Arab revolt against the Ottomans. This correspondence, during 1915–16, held out the possibility of an Arab state, though the correspondence was inconclusive and no agreement was ever signed. One reason for this was that Britain was also aware of France's interest in the area of Syria and Lebanon. It had placed a caveat in its negotiations with Hussein that France's interests could not be ignored, which Hussein did not wish to give. The United States had not been party to these secret agreements and, as a result, refused to recognize their validity [*Doc. 4*]. The American position was complicated by the fact that while it had broken diplomatic relations with the Ottoman Empire it had never declared war upon it and therefore, technically, should not need to be involved in peace negotiations.

In addition to those already promised a share of the spoils expected to be carved out of the prostrate Ottoman Empire, Greece also laid claim to those areas of Asia Minor which possessed significant Greek ethnic populations. Large stretches of the Aegean coast of Anatolia contained substantial Greek populations who were referred to as the 'unredeemed' Greeks. The collapse of Ottoman power had opened the way for Greece to pursue what had been a central object of its foreign policy for several decades, the *Megali Idea* (Great Idea), which envisaged uniting all the Greek populated areas into a single Greater Greece. Some Greeks even dreamt of re-establishing the Byzantine empire with its capital at Constantinople. The Greek premier, Venizelos, had worked assiduously during the war and at the peace conference to build good relations with the key Allied powers so as to obtain support for these plans.

FROM THE MUDROS ARMISTICE TO THE TREATY OF SÈVRES

The secret treaties had, in part, been an attempt to settle the most contentious issues concerning the future disposition of the territories of the Ottoman Empire. This turned out not to be the case but rather, a cause for dispute among the wartime Allies. Italy hoped to create an Aegean empire, having previously seized the Dodecanese islands in 1911 and the important mainland port of Antalya at the end of the war. The 1915 Treaty of London had promised Italy, in vague terms, a sphere of influence around Antalya. Italian troops were landed at several strategic places along the coast in preparation for a move to take Smyrna. This city also formed the centre of Greek ambitions. The other members of the Council of Four began to fear that Italy would attempt to preempt its decisions by occupying more of Anatolia, moving out from its mainland foothold in the direction of the key city of Smyrna. With all their forces fully deployed the Allies decided to take advantage of these conflicting Greco-Italian ambitions to force Italy not to act unilaterally. In May 1919 the Allied powers authorized Greece to occupy Smyrna. The Greek landing did indeed succeed in forestalling Italy, but it simultaneously ignited a Turkish nationalist reaction which was to have far-reaching consequences. The new communist government in Russia had already published the secret treaties, which they had found among the papers of the previous regime. This event, combined with the Allies' support for the Greek occupation around Smyrna, provided Turkish nationalists with ample proof of Allied intentions.

Turkish resistance was now rallied by one of the country's most successful generals, Mustafa Kemal (later surnamed Atatürk), who would become the most famous figure of twentieth-century Turkey. Kemal would later observe of that fateful landing of the Greeks at Smyrna, 'If the enemy had not stupidly come here, the whole country might have slept on heedlessly.'[1] Within days Kemal set about uniting the dispersed Turkish resistance. The army, together with many Turks throughout the country, rallied to him and he and his supporters subscribed to a 'National Pact' which vowed to preserve the integrity of the Turkish-speaking portions of the Ottoman Empire. It is noteworthy that the Nationalists laid no claim to the non-Turkish portions of the Empire, mostly lying south of the Tarsus mountains in the Middle East, recognizing that there was no chance of regaining them. This allowed the new movement to harness Turkish nationalism, moving away from the more diverse identity of the Ottoman Empire. By the end of 1919 Kemal's supporters were in control of most of Turkey, with the exception of Constantinople and the contiguous area along the Straits, where the Sultan remained the notional ruler due to the Allied occupation, and the Greek enclave around Smyrna.

The Allies, concerned by the potential threat to their plans posed by the growing Nationalist movement, now hurried to complete the peace treaty with the Sultan's government, the last of the peace treaties to be concluded. The terms of the treaty were made public in May 1920, though the treaty was not signed until August at Sèvres, near Paris. By its terms Greece received significant territorial gains in Thrace and Asia Minor, receiving Adrianople (Edirne), the strategically valuable islands of Imbros and Tenedos, and control of the Smyrna district for five years after which a plebiscite would be held on its incorporation into Greece. In addition, two new states were created and initially intended to be League of Nations mandates: Armenia and Kurdistan. The Ottoman Empire's Middle Eastern provinces became League of Nations Mandates. Britain received the mandates for Palestine and Iraq, with the oil-rich district of Mosul being added to Iraq. France received Lebanon and Syria, with control of the area around Adana in Turkey. Italy's sphere of influence over the Antalya area was confirmed, as was its sovereignty over the Dodecanese islands. The Straits were opened to all shipping at all times and placed under the control of an International Straits Commission, dominated by Britain, France, Italy, and Japan. Turkey, in common with the other defeated Central Powers, was to pay reparations and its army was limited to 50,000 soldiers. War criminals were to be handed over to the League of Nations for trial. By concluding a peace treaty with the Sultan's government, rather than with Kemal's Nationalists, the Allies became committed to attempting to preserve the monarchy against the revolutionary movement led by Kemal. By obliging the sultan to sign such a harsh treaty, however, they simultaneously seriously undermined what authority he had left. The Turks now had two governments, the decayed sultanate under Allied occupation and the nationalist movement led by Kemal.

THE GREEK-TURKISH WAR

The Nationalists reacted vigorously to the terms of the treaty, including making some forays against British positions. At the time Britain was distracted by uprisings in Ireland and Egypt, tension with Afghanistan which had led to a brief war in 1919, and an extremely volatile situation in British-ruled India. France was tied down by events in Syria. Britain and France, therefore, decided to turn to Greece for assistance in dealing with the Nationalists. Greek forces now moved out from the Smyrna enclave, initially with great success. The situation for Greece changed dramatically, however, when one of those quirks of fate, with which history is replete, intervened to change the course of events. In October 1920 King Alexander of Greece died after being bitten by a pet monkey. This led to a general election in which the architect of Greece's wartime diplomacy, Venizelos, suffered a surprise defeat and left the country, opening the way for the return of Alexander's exiled father, King Constantine, who had been driven from the throne in 1916 by Venizelos on the dubious pretext of pro-German sympathies. Whatever the reality of Constantine's sympathies, he was viewed by the Allies with profound suspicion and his return to Athens led to a dramatic decline in pro-Greek sentiment among the Allies. The new royalist government was viewed as untrustworthy, and memories of its supposed wartime pro-German sympathies led to its being treated as virtually an enemy government. Overnight the perception of Greece shifted from that of loyal ally, under the venerated Venizelos, to that of a pariah state under a king, already once deposed with Allied connivance.

The new Greek royalist government proceeded to purge the army of Venizelist officers, weakening its efficiency at a critical time. The Greek government, however, was determined to maintain Greece's position in Anatolia, and a series of offensives were mounted against the Nationalist forces between January and August 1921, pushing them back to the Sakkaria River. The Turkish line here was the last obstacle before Ankara, the Nationalist headquarters, some forty miles away, but as events proved it was also the high water mark of the Greek advance. The Battle of the Sakkaria River saw Kemal brilliantly envelop the Greek army. The Turkish counter-offensive shattered the Greek army which fled towards Smyrna, where inadequate planning trapped many of the soldiers. Smyrna fell to the Nationalist army, and most of the Greek sections of the city were burned, with many Greek deaths. This event effectively ended the war. The debacle sent over one million refugees fleeing to Greece. King Constantine abdicated and, subsequently, the new Greek government tried and executed five ex-ministers for their part in the disaster. The Greek defeat became known in Greek history as the 'catastrophe'.

FROM THE CHANAK CRISIS TO THE TREATY OF LAUSANNE

In the wake of the signature of the Sèvres treaty, with domestic support for them rapidly increasing, the Nationalists gained international credibility as a force in Turkish politics. In March 1921 the Soviet government recognized the Nationalist government and concluded a Soviet-Turkish treaty of Friendship. Initially, it had been difficult for Kemal to communicate with other governments due to his geographical isolation and British command of the seas. Lying between Russia and Turkey was the newly independent Armenian republic, which was deeply hostile to Turkey and which aspired to annex the parts of historic Armenia under Turkish control. The Armenian republic had provided a base for raids on border villages and this, in turn, led the Turkish nationalist forces to attack the Armenian republic. The Turks succeeded in capturing Kars and Ardahan, and peace was concluded with Armenia by the Treaty of Alexandropol in November 1920. This opened the way for communication with the Russian government and, as a result, Soviet Russia became the first state to recognize the Ankara government. Because of these links Kemal was suspected at the time of being a Soviet fellow traveller, which in fact was not the case, but this increased suspicion on the part of the Allies helps to explain why they were so reluctant to deal with him.

Lloyd George had consistently pursued a strongly pro-Greek policy and, although disappointed by the fall of Venizelos, he hoped that the defeat of the Greek royalist army at the hand of the Turkish Nationalists would see the restoration of a friendly government in Greece. As a result Lloyd George continued to oppose the Nationalists. The French, meanwhile, had begun diverging from cooperation with Britain. In March 1921 the French negotiated an agreement with Kemal, by which the Nationalists committed themselves to repaying Turkey's prewar bonds, which were mostly due to French holders. In return France evacuated its forces from Turkey. Later the same month Italy made a similar agreement.

Kemal, after his defeat of the Greeks, had set his sights on taking Constantinople, a possibility enhanced by his agreements with France and Italy. The French and Italians had withdrawn their garrisons from Constantinople in September 1921 and Britain was, therefore, now alone in defending both the Sèvres settlement and Constantinople, where it had a small force deployed. Constantinople and the key points on the Straits remained in British hands, and British seapower assured control of these coastal areas through the presence of its powerful Mediterranean fleet. In September 1922 Nationalist soldiers crossed the Dardanelles with the goal of driving Greek forces from eastern Thrace. In so doing they entered the British-declared neutral zone near the strategically important Chanak peninsula. Lloyd George was determined to defend Constantinople and called upon the support of the British dominions. He was supported by the hawks in his cabinet, among them Churchill, but was opposed by the foreign secretary, Curzon. It seemed, at that moment, as if a major war was about to erupt. Kemal, though, proved himself not only to be a brilliant general but a sagacious political strategist. He knew when to push and when to be moderate. Having displayed his potential military power he agreed to talks in October at Mudania. An agreement was quickly reached that allowed the Nationalist forces to enter eastern Thrace, on the

European side of the Straits, and it was agreed that the Treaty of Sèvres would be renegotiated. As a result of this agreement Turkey would become the only one of the defeated Central Powers to succeed in challenging the terms imposed upon it.

The Chanak Crisis, which had threatened war, proved the last straw for Lloyd George's coalition government. Bonar Law, leader of the Conservative Party, complained that Britain could not alone act as the policeman of the world. The Conservatives withdrew from the coalition and Lloyd George, the architect of Britain's victory in the First World War, was forced to resign. He was replaced by a Conservative government led by Bonar Law. A further consequence of the crisis was that Britain's self-governing dominions, concerned that they might have been hastily committed to war over a crisis obscure to their interests, began to demand greater independence. This was the turning point in Britain's relations with these countries and would lead to their full independence under an agreement reached at the 1926 Imperial Conference and confirmed by the Statute of Westminster in 1931.

At the end of October 1922 the Nationalists took control of Constantinople and, in November, abolished the monarchy. A few days later the last Ottoman sultan fled into exile aboard HMS *Malaya* and a new era in Turkish history began. Kemal was careful to have a gradual transition, and Mehmed's heir Abdulmecid, was allowed to assume the historic title of caliph, symbolic of leadership of the Islamic world. In 1924 even this vestige of the old imperial regime was abolished and a republic was proclaimed, with Kemal as its first president.

The new Conservative British government now faced the task of negotiating a new peace with Turkey. Lord Curzon continued as foreign secretary in the new cabinet and was a key figure in the peace negotiations conducted at Lausanne, in neutral Switzerland. Here the parties to the redundant Sèvres treaty met the representatives of the Nationalist Turkish forces and, after much tough negotiating, reached a settlement [*Doc. 15*]. By the Treaty of Lausanne (24 July 1923), which superseded the earlier Treaty of Sèvres, Turkey confirmed its loss of the Arab portions of the Ottoman Empire, but regained control from Greece of the strategic Aegean islands of Imbros and Tenedos, as well as eastern Thrace. The right enjoyed by citizens of the major European states to extraterritoriality, known as the capitulations, was abolished and it was agreed that Turkey would not have to pay reparations. The plans for separate Armenian and Kurdish states embodied in the Sèvres treaty were dropped. The Straits remained open to all commercial traffic, the number of naval vessels of non-riparian states in the Black Sea at any one time was restricted and, if Turkey was at war, only neutral ships would be allowed to pass. The application of these regulations was entrusted to an International Commission of the Straits reporting to the League of Nations. These provisions were later superseded by the 1936

Montreux Convention. Greece and Turkey agreed to an exchange of populations, with 400,000 Turks being sent to Turkey, in exchange for 1.3 million Greeks. For Greece the influx of refugees from both the war in Anatolia and those exchanged by Turkey proved a vast strain upon the economy and underlay a difficult domestic political scene for years to come.

One thorny issue was left by the Lausanne treaty to be settled by the League of Nations, the future of the potentially oil-rich region of Mosul, which lay between the new Turkey and the British-administered Mesopotamia mandate. This area was predominantly Kurdish and, as the Turkish National Pact claimed sovereignty over non-Arab Muslim regions, it therefore included this region. Kemal hoped that the Kurdish population already within Turkey could be assimilated, a task which would be made much more difficult if a substantial Kurdish culture remained outside Turkey's frontiers. Britain, however, wanted to see this area, potentially rich in oil, coming within its sphere. It was agreed to refer the matter to the League of Nations. Eventually, in 1925, the League awarded most of the disputed territory to Mesopotamia. The Kurds, thus, were spread over the territory of Turkey, Iraq, Iran, and Soviet Russia and their quest for an independent Kurdistan remains a vexatious issue in international relations.

THE MIDDLE EAST

In the Middle East during the war an Arab national revolt in 1916, combined with a British attack from Egypt, drove out the Ottoman regime. Jerusalem fell to the British in 1917 and Ottoman forces were finally defeated at the battle of Megiddo in September 1918. The Mudros armistice found Britain in occupation of most of the former Ottoman Middle East. At the peace conference its fate would cause great tension between Britain and France, which had been traditional rivals for dominance in the region. There were also local aspirants to control, with both Arabs and Jews hoping to gain control of some part of the former Ottoman lands.

After the Ottoman Empire's entry into the war the British High Commissioner in Egypt, McMahon, had begun secret correspondence with the Emir Hussein, head of the Hashemite clan who controlled the Muslim Holy City of Mecca. Britain hoped that an Arab popular revolt would cause a serious diversion for the Ottoman army. Britan held out a hope in the McMahon–Hussein correspondence of a future Arab state led by Hussein, though it reserved the area west of Damascus as a reward for France, and lower Iraq for itself. The Arab revolt began in June 1916 led by Hussein's son, Faisal and, though it enjoyed limited success, it achieved its purpose, from Britain's perspective, of tying down Ottoman forces and, from Hussein's side, it added to the importance of his family, positioning them to become the leaders of the Arab cause.

The issue was further complicated by an intra-Arab dispute. The Emir Hussein dreamt of uniting the Arabs under his rule and had been instrumental in the Arab revolt which had done so much to remove Ottoman rule. Initially, he had attempted to assume the title 'King of the Arabs', but was forced by the Allies to adopt the more modest style of King of the Hejaz, the region around Mecca. In this region, though, Hussein faced opposition from Ibn Saud, leader of the puritanical Wahabi Muslims. Here, the vast geographical interests of the British Empire brought it into conflict with itself. The British Government of India supported Ibn Saud, while Hussein enjoyed support from the British authorities in Cairo. The British viceroy in India was concerned that the Arab national revolt could prove a dangerous precedent in India, while the British administration in Egypt was focused on the immediate issue of defeating the Ottoman army. In 1919 Hussein's and Ibn Saud's forces fought a number of battles and skirmishes, each having been supplied with British arms. The incident illustrates the difficulty of coordinating policy in an empire that straddled the globe. The rivalry between Hussein and Ibn Saud continued; Ibn Saud slowly gained the upper hand, taking Mecca in late 1924 and, by the end of 1925, gaining control of most of the Arabian peninsula. Subsequently, he renamed the country he controlled Saudi Arabia. The Hashemites, with their ambitions thwarted in Arabia, sought outlets elsewhere in the Middle East.

At the end of the war Hussein's son, Faisal, had occupied the Syrian capital, Damascus, on behalf of the Allies. Faisal hoped that this could be used as the core of a new Arab kingdom. Faisal was present at the Paris Peace Conference, but it was made clear to him that he represented only his father's small state of the Hejaz, and not a wider Arab state. Faisal argued the Arab case on the basis of Wilson's pledge of national self-determination and suggested a commission of inquiry. Wilson happily accepted the idea but Britain and France, with aspirations to control the region themselves, did not. In the end only two American commissioners visited the region, producing the King–Crane report for the peace conference. King and Crane travelled through Syria and Palestine during the summer of 1919, and it is likely that local British officials were able to exert some control over whom they interviewed. The report concluded that: the population of the region did not wish to become a League mandate as this was viewed as merely another form of imperial rule, though some transitional arrangement was acceptable as a preparation for full independence. The King–Crane report concluded that the local inhabitants preferred any help to come from the United States, would accept Britain if necessary, and definitely did not want France. As a result Britain and France chose to ignore the report, while Wilson by that time was not in a position to press for the report's consideration. The Allies, as a result, proceeded with their plans to divide control of the Middle East.

In an effort to preempt this Faisal, upon his return from the peace conference in the spring of 1919, had organized the election of a national congress to meet at Damascus. In November he reached a pragmatic compromise with France that left France in control of the coast, with a commitment that France alone would provide assistance to the new Syrian state. Faisal could not persuade the other Arab leaders to accept this and in March 1920 the congress declared Syria's independence with Faisal as king. It was intended that this new Syria would also include Palestine and an autonomous Lebanon. At the same time, Iraq declared its independence with Faisal's brother, Abdullah, as king.

The following month the Allies, meeting at San Remo, decided upon the distribution of the new League of Nations mandates for the region assigning Syria and Lebanon to France, and Palestine and Iraq to Britain. The Palestine mandate included a provision for Britain to create a Jewish homeland there. In July 1920 some of Faisal's forces attacked French positions in Lebanon and, in response, France decided to resolve the situation by force, occupying Syria in July 1920 and expelling the erstwhile king. There were, however, other thrones to be won and Faisal was not long without one.

Britain, which was already facing the strains of a globally dispersed empire and with few resources it could deploy in the new mandates, sought ways of minimizing the demands upon its resources that these mandates would cause. Churchill travelled to Cairo in March 1921 where a conference was held among the British officials. It was decided that it would be most effective to govern Britain's Arab mandates by placing them in the nominal charge of an Arab ruler who, it was hoped, would assure the support and loyalty of the predominantly Arab populations, though would be subject to the advice of British High Commissioners and a small British military and administrative presence. It was decided to offer Faisal the throne of Iraq, and his brother Abdullah the throne of Transjordan. The latter state was officially part of the Palestine mandate, but did not include that part designated to form a Jewish national home.

The plan for a Jewish national homeland in the ancient Holy Land had been an aspiration of many Jews, and their non-Jewish supporters, for some time. The viscious oppression of many Jewish populations in the nineteenth century, particularly in Russia and other eastern European states, had led to discussion about finding a safe haven for these populations. Eventually, the idea of a return to their ancient homeland became the favoured option and a Zionist movement emerged. This idea also appealed to many in British government circles as a way both to block French ambitions and create a British dependent buffer for the Suez Canal. As the war progressed it was thought an official pronouncement to this effect would also be useful public diplomacy, particularly in the United States, and in November 1917 the

British Foreign Secretary, Balfour, expressed Britain's views in what has become known as the Balfour Declaration [*Doc. 1*]. While the declaration did not expressly state that Britain would assume the oversight of any such settlement, it was clearly an aspiration of many British policy makers.

The French opted to rule their mandate directly through a high commissioner. Traditionally, France had interests in the predominantly Christian Mount Lebanon area around Beirut, which had been an autonomous district of the Ottoman Empire since 1861. France now extended Lebanon to include predominantly Muslim Tripoli and the Bekaa valley, thus altering the religious balance of the country. Decades later these changes would become the basis for the Lebanon Crisis that erupted in 1976. As with the imposition of British rule in its Middle East mandates, the Arab population was unhappy and a revolt broke out in 1925 against French rule that simmered for two years.

Britain was forced to review its relationship with Egypt as a result of the First World War. Egypt had been theoretically part of the Ottoman Empire until the war, but was really under British domination. With the outbreak of war Britain had declared Egypt independent of the Ottoman Empire and a British protectorate. The events of the war and growing frustration with British dominance led to a rising in 1919, one of several such events throughout Britain's empire in that year which led to a severe overstretching of its military resources. It became clear to the British that to continue the existing arrangement was to court a full-scale revolt. In 1922, therefore, the protectorate was abolished and the independence of Egypt recognized, subject to certain safeguards for British interests. This was not sufficient to assuage nationalist feeling and led to the assassination in 1924 of Sir Lee Stack, British commander of the Egyptian army, who served simultaneously as governor-general of Sudan, at that time an Anglo-Egyptian condominium. Britain retaliated by imposing a large financial penalty upon Egypt. The situation would oscillate in subsequent years between tension and moderate cooperation, culminating in the 1956 Suez Crisis which saw the Egyptian expropriation of the Suez Canal and the ending of Britain's special position in Egypt.

CONCLUSION

The Eastern Question, that long-running problem of international relations over the fate of the Ottoman Empire, now seemed to have been resolved. The political geography of the eastern Mediterranean was transformed. The successor states of the Ottoman Empire would, however, prove a volatile mix in the decades to follow and would engage the diplomatic attention of the Great Powers. Greece, after a brief bid to restore itself to the glory of the old Byzantine empire, was forced back and a new Turkish republic emerged with a strong sense of national identity. Relations between these two states were to remain peaceful until the 1950s but the animosities that had culminated in the Greek-Turkish War of 1919–22, together with the severity of its impact, would ensure that this would be a tense relationship for the remainder of the century. In the Middle East Britain and France emerged as the predominant powers but, although they remained cooperative on many issues elsewhere, in the Middle East they would remain regional rivals. Both Britain and France had been severely drained by the war and they had few resources to spare for these newly acquired Middle Eastern realms. The mandates would increasingly become a drag on Britain and France as they were confronted by a rising tide of opposition from the inhabitants. The eastern Mediterranean world would remain a problem area in international relations as much after the war as it had during the century which had preceded it. In many ways the postwar settlement only marked a new phase of the old Eastern Question.

Note

1   A. Mango, *Atatürk* (London, 2000), p. 217.

CHAPTER SEVEN

NAVAL RIVALRY AND EAST ASIAN STABILITY

One of the most serious areas of international tension after the First World War was East Asia. Very little relating to it had actually been resolved at the Paris Peace Conference and the trajectory of conflicting ambitions and naval rivalry in the Pacific, abetted by mounting political turmoil in China, made this a potential area of conflict between some of the Great Powers. Japan's growing strength was bringing it increasingly into conflict with the other rising non-European power, the United States. Britain was caught in the midst of this friction as it was allied, on the one hand, to Japan but, on the other, seeking a closer relationship with America. The immediate cause for concern was the growing likelihood of a naval arms race involving these three states. After the destruction of the German navy only these three countries possessed navies with significant power. All were Pacific basin states and, thus, the questions of naval strength and the Pacific balance of power became inextricably linked. The problem was solved, at least for much of the decade of the 1920s, through the favored mechanism of postwar diplomacy, the holding of a conference. The Washington Conference of 1921–22, through a network of agreements, established a framework for naval arms control, the first ever voluntary agreement for such a purpose, and established parameters for the Great Powers' relations with China.

THE RISE OF JAPANESE POWER

Just as the war in Europe had seen a change in the relationship of the traditional regional actors, so the war had also affected the balance of power in East Asia. Japan took the opportunity to continue its drive for regional dominance that had been slowly increasing since its dramatic and rapid modernization in the mid-nineteenth century. In 1895 it had defeated China and taken the island of Taiwan. In 1902 it had formed an alliance with Britain, the first such peacetime alliance concluded by either state. In 1905 it had inflicted a stunning defeat on the Russian Empire, seizing control of Port Arthur (Lushun), a key Russian naval base leased from

China. The defeat of Russia and the growing weakness of China opened the way for Japan to annex Korea in 1910. During the First World War, true to its alliance with Britain, Japan declared war on Germany in 1914. Its fleet played an important part in driving German power from the Pacific and, in return, it was able to seize the German-ruled Shantung (Shandong) peninsula and the German Pacific islands north of the equator. China had been forced to grant Germany a ninety-nine year lease on the Shantung peninsula in 1897. At its tip lay the great German-built fortress of Tsingtao (Qingdao) which guarded the entrance to Kiaochow bay, home to the German Pacific fleet. Among its many assets was one of the largest dry docks in the world. The siege of Tsingtao in 1914 was the only major land battle in East Asia during the war and gave Japan a prize strategic asset.

Japan had gradually been strengthening its position in China. China had historically been the regional great power, but it had been in decline for much of the last century. The 1911 Chinese Revolution had left an already weakened country in turmoil. In 1915 Japan presented the Chinese government with an ultimatum, the 'twenty-one demands', that would give Japan control of Shantung, southern Manchuria, inner Mongolia, and various mineral exploitation rights. The coast along Fukien would become a Japanese sphere of influence and China would utilize Japanese political, military and financial advisers. The Chinese government, powerless to resist, was compelled to agree to all but the last point. Japan further extended its regional hegemony when Russia withdrew from the war after the Bolshevik seizure of power. Japan was able to take control of Russia's Pacific maritime provinces as part of the Allied intervention into Russia. After the war ended and the other Allies withdrew their forces Japan remained, strengthening its hold on the region. The growth of Japan's power had been such that by the time of the First World War it was viewed as a Great Power and at the Paris Peace Conference it was accorded that status, being treated on equal terms with Great Britain, France, Italy, and the United States.

China, at this time, was in a state of flux. A revolution in 1911 led by Sun Yat-sen had ended the monarchy and attempted to establish a republic. By 1915, however, China was dissolving into political chaos, with various local figures effectively controlling their own regions. In 1917 the political crisis in China had reached the stage that there were rival governments, which split the country between north and south, with one government based at Peking (Beijing) and a rival parliamentary government at Canton. In addition local warlords emerged who would come to control many parts of the country, though it should be noted that none of these were separatist groups and the idea of a single China never disappeared. In 1918, as the First World War was drawing to a close, the officially recognized government based at Peking entered the war on the side of the Allies, largely to assure itself of a place at the eventual peace conference. As an indication of some national unity the Canton government indicated its support of this action a month later.

Japan's bid to become the regional hegemon was opposed by the United States. In 1917, after American entry into the war, Japan sent a mission to Washington to see if an understanding on this matter could be reached. The Japanese representative, Viscount Ishii, and the American secretary of state, Robert Lansing, reached an accord that became known as the Lansing–Ishii agreement, recognizing that Japan did have special interests in China. This agreement was interpreted differently by both parties, with Lansing believing that it applied to economic interests, while Japan viewed it as an acknowledgement of a Japanese sphere of influence over southern Manchuria. It is possible that Lansing acted as he did believing it to be necessary to keep Japan in the war and on the side of the Allies. The contradictory interpretations of the parties, however, further worsened relations.

After the war Japan continued an active naval building programme that looked likely to make it the regional maritime power, something which concerned the United States as it had its own regional presence based in the Philippines, which it had captured from Spain in 1899. By 1920 military expenditure constituted 48 per cent of Japanese governmental expenditure. As Japan continued its naval construction, while simultaneously building up its presence on the mainland, the twin issues of the future of China and the potential naval arms race came to dominate international concerns over East Asia in the years immediately after the war.

THE PARIS PEACE CONFERENCE AND THE SIBERIAN AFFAIR

Japan's representative to the Paris Peace Conference was Saionji, the youngest of its recognized elder statesmen. Although included in the discussions of the Council of Ten, he limited his interventions to issues of specific interest to Japan: the future of Shantung, the control of Germany's Pacific island possessions, and racial equality. Shantung proved to be a significant issue. China's delegation, led by Wellington Koo, argued that the 1915 agreement, by which Japan had taken Shantung, was invalid as it was made under the threat of force. While legally dubious China's argument attracted sympathy from the United States. Britain attempted to find a solution that kept both its important allies happy by proposing that Japan control Shantung as a League of Nations mandate. Japan rejected this and, in the end, succeeded in establishing in the Treaty of Versailles its succession to Germany's former rights in China, subject to any arrangements it subsequently made with China. News of the rejection of Chinese aspirations led to public protests in China, which became known from the date of this as the May 4th movement. The public outcry was sufficient to lead to the Cabinet in Peking resigning and China's refusal to sign the treaty. As a result this left Japan in control of Shantung *de facto* but not *de jure*.

During the war, when British naval forces were seriously stretched, it had requested Japanese assistance, which led to Japan sending destroyers to the Mediterranean. In return Japan received a promise of support from Britain, France, and Italy for Japan's ambition to gain permanent control of Germany's former Pacific island possessions, north of the equator. The United States had not been party to this understanding and refused to be bound by any of the wartime secret treaties. A compromise was finally agreed at the peace conference that these islands would be awarded to Japan as a League of Nations mandate, while those south of the equator were also assigned as mandates to Great Britain, Australia, and New Zealand.

One area in which Japanese hopes failed was its desire for a racial equality clause to be incorporated in the Covenant of the League of Nations. One of the issues confronting Japan in the early part of the twentieth century was the treatment of its emigrants. Australia and the United States had imposed targeted restrictions on immigration from Japan. Population pressure in Japan had led many Japanese to seek opportunities overseas and restrictions such as these were a matter of concern to the Japanese government. In February 1919 Baron Makino, Japan's member of the committee drafting the covenant, proposed such a clause and received support from China, Czechoslovakia, France, Greece, and Poland. The Australian prime minister, Hughes, strongly objected and in April 1919 both Australia and the United States (the latter because of pressure primarily from California) ensured its defeat. Although Japan went on to be a permanent member of the League Council this defeat remained an irritant.

An issue that caused some tension with Japan's allies was the Siberian affair. Within weeks of the Bolshevik seizure of power the Japanese army was preparing plans to intervene in Siberia to prevent the spread of communist influence to China, which it feared could undermine its influence there. The foreign ministry quite independently evolved similar plans, though in this instance out of concern about German intentions. This incident shows some of the problems of decision-making in Japan, with difficulties of coordination. Once a common plan was agreed Japan sought the support of its allies, but the United States objected, convinced that Japan was intending to use this opportunity to extend its sphere of influence. It was only when the Czech Legion had fought its way across Siberia and seized the port of Vladivostock that Wilson, reluctantly, agreed to a limited intervention in order to extricate the Czechs. The Japanese government agreed, promising to limit its deployment to one or possibly two divisions. The army, however, planned on seven divisions and despite assurances to the contrary the army plan is what occurred. By the 1930s the inability of the Japanese government to control the army would become a serious issue, but this move, unpopular both at home and abroad, provides an illustration of what would become a growing problem for the control of Japan's external policy. Japanese forces fanned out to take control of a vast area. Eventually branches of Japan's large industrial concerns, the *zaibatsu*, were opened in this region and some 50,000 Japanese settlers began to arrive. This growing presence increasingly became a problem for Japan with its wartime allies, who ended their military intervention in early 1920.

NAVAL ARMAMENTS AND STABILITY IN EAST ASIA

Among the three powerful naval states, the United States, Britain, and Japan there was a looming naval arms race that would have dwarfed the proportions of the prewar Anglo-German naval arms rivalry. Given the technology of the period the heart of this rivalry lay in the construction of huge capital ships, that is those ships that displaced more than 10,000 tons and carried guns of calibres in excess of eight inches. Ships of this type were usually termed either battleships or battle cruisers. In 1918 Britain had launched HMS *Hood* which displaced 41,200 tons and, despite its size, could also move with remarkable speed. Both the United States and Japan were at work on similar monster-sized capital ships.

The United States was deeply concerned by the Anglo-Japanese alliance, which fell due for renewal in 1921. There was concern in Washington at the potential security threat posed by a combination of these two great naval powers. Between 1917 and 1921 Japanese naval expenditure had almost tripled and was still increasing, while Britain's Royal Navy remained the world's largest. If, for any reason, the Anglo-Japanese alliance turned on the United States their fleets would pose a deadly threat to American security. President Wilson had already begun to build the basis for American maritime security in the 1916 Navy Bill, when he called for a navy second to none. This bill initiated the construction of 156 ships, including 16 battleships or battle cruisers. Priority was given during the war to construction of the smaller categories of ships. As a result, capital ship construction was only reaching its peak in 1921 when 15 of the 16 envisaged capital ships were under construction.

The incoming Republican administration of President Harding was confronted by a number of issues. While the Republicans had attacked membership of the League of Nations due its collective security obligations, they did want to be seen dealing positively with matters for which the League might have provided a venue for negotiation, in particular arms control. The new administration was under strong pressure to lower taxes which, in turn, would require less government expenditure. As a result, there was growing opposition in the Congress to paying for the expensive naval construction programme. After the 1920 election one of the leading opponents of membership of the League, Senator Borah, proposed a resolution for a 50 per cent reduction in the naval construction of the United States, Britain, and Japan. The Borah resolution received a tidal wave of public support and was passed unanimously by the Senate, placing great pressure on the administration to find a way to reduce spending while assuring security.

For Britain one of the most satisfying outcomes of the First World War was the destruction of Germany's navy, which had once seemed to pose a great threat. By November 1918 the Royal Navy had achieved a tonnage and number of ships nearly equal to all the remaining major fleets of the world. The Royal Navy, now at the apogee of its power, numbered 61 battleships, a navy greater than that of the United States and France combined, and double that of Japan's and Italy's. British naval doctrine called for a navy based on a two-power standard, that is a navy greater than the next two largest navies combined. The American building programme threatened this. Financial constraints prohibited Britain from attempting to maintain a two-power standard against the United States and the doctrine was downgraded to a one-power standard. Britain, in considering its own security, could not accept the United States creating a larger navy than its own. As a result the British government, in March 1921, reluctantly authorized a new building programme. It was anxious, however, not to embark on a new naval arms race if it could possibly be avoided. It had stopped large-scale naval construction with the end of the war and had tried to reach an arms control agreement with the United States on several occasions. It was only when confronted with the spectre of continued American construction that a decision was taken to embark on construction of a new generation of super battle cruisers.

The United States and Britain, therefore, were facing an expensive naval arms race if they maintained their existing plans. Neither, however, expected to face immediate conflict with the other, especially in the aftermath of their close relationship during the war. Both governments also faced strong domestic pressure to cut defence spending in order to reduce taxes and to focus on domestic concerns. American hesitation turned on the Anglo-Japanese alliance. While not viewing an attack by Britain as likely, the United States did believe that it provided important support for Japanese expansionism. The issue of whether or not to renew the alliance became the chief topic for the 1921 Imperial Conference, a gathering that brought together all the prime ministers of the British dominions.

This was the first gathering of the leaders of the British Empire's dominions since the Paris Peace Conference. In considering the world situation two years on they were confident of the empire's strong position. The ebullient Billy Hughes of Australia exclaimed, 'We are like so many

Alexanders. What other worlds have we to conquer?', while the more judicious Jan Smuts of South Africa observed that the British Empire 'emerged from the war quite the greatest Power in the world, and it is only unwisdom or unsound policy that could rob her of that great position.'[1] The looming crisis over the renewal of the Japanese alliance, and the potential impact on Anglo-American relations was one of the few immediate issues which might threaten that hard-won security. The alliance with Japan had first been concluded in 1902 out of common concern over the growth of Russian power in East Asia, it had been renewed in 1911 out of concern about the growing German role in the region. The alliance had served both partners well during its life, but now the interests of the partners were more clearly divergent than previously. It was clearly an unsympathetic alliance, with little sense of common purpose. Britain, too, was concerned at Japan's move towards regional hegemony as well as growing economic competition. There was concern over Japanese envy of Britain's worldwide empire, which invited comparison to Germany's prewar jealousy that had caused so much friction. Some members of the Imperial Conference argued that the alliance provided Britain with some measure of influence and control over Japan. Others pointed out that the growing divergence of Japan and the United States made renewal a potential further cause of difficulty with the United States [*Doc. 13*]. The Imperial Conference split along regional lines, with the Australian and New Zealand premiers wanting to do nothing to antagonize Japan, while Canada was concerned not to alienate the United States.

British links with the United States had been growing for a number of years. The interconnections of the two countries were among the most complex of the great powers, bound not only by language and a shared history, but also by financial ties and networks of personal friendships and family bonds. Britain may have sought amity and cooperation with the United States in principle, but in practice there were many obstacles. One concern was the financial problem between the two countries. The Wilson administration in its last days had been adamant on repayment of Britain's war debt. The Harding administration had only taken office in March 1921, and Britain hoped to take the opportunity to establish a good relationship that could lead to a resolution of the current set of problems between them and later, during the Washington Conference period, it never forgot the need to try to ameliorate the debt question.

An important step in working with the new administration in Washington was to ascertain its view about the Anglo-Japanese alliance. The message from Washington was clear, with the new Secretary of State, Charles Evans Hughes, informing the British ambassador that he viewed any renewal of the alliance with 'disquietude'. For Britain the conundrum lay in the reality that, as the United States traditionally avoided peacetime alliances (and continued to do so until the 1949 NATO treaty), there was little possibility of replacing the Japanese alliance with an American one. Britain, therefore, had to decide between retaining the reality of its relationship with Japan, despite its growing concerns about the increasingly predatory nature of Japanese diplomacy, and the danger inherent in antagonizing the United States, which at the very least would result in an expensive naval arms race which Britain could not hope to win. It was projected that by 1923 America, at its current construction rate, would possess a larger navy than Britain's. Under severe economic pressure after the war, Britain could ill afford unnecessary military expenditure.

The Imperial Conference agreed, being unable to decide otherwise, to leave the issue of the Anglo-Japanese alliance open for the moment and, in the meantime, to make a further effort with the United States. In the light of a new administration and clear American public sentiment for arms reduction, Britain hoped that a solution could be negotiated. The problems of the renewal of the Anglo-Japanese alliance and the naval arms race now converged. Britain approached the American government and suggested the United States convene a conference on naval arms control, and this came to be broadened out to cover the linked issues of East Asia and the Pacific.

THE WASHINGTON CONFERENCE

It is often argued that the United States became isolationist after the First World War and the rejection of membership in the League of Nations. In fact the United States remained an active international actor, as witnessed by its hosting a major international conference only a little over two years after the signature of the Treaty of Versailles. The Washington Conference convened in November 1921 and was dominated from the start by Secretary of State Hughes. He dramatically seized the initiative in the opening session by proposing a definite plan for naval arms reduction [*Doc. 14*]. He suggested that the navies of the great maritime powers be governed by a ratio in order to avoid future expensive arms races, a ten-year naval building holiday, and an agreement on the total naval shipping tonnage to be allowed and to be achieved, if necessary, by the scrapping of ships to achieve those totals. The Hughes plan would have resulted in the scrapping of 66 ships by the United States, Britain, and Japan. In a modified form the Hughes plan would ultimately be adopted by the conference.

Hughes had suggested a ratio of 5-5-3 between the United States, Britain, and Japan, with 1.7 each for France and Italy. This was based, roughly, on existing naval strengths. Japan protested at what it considered the implied inferiority, with one Japanese delegate stating that to him it sounded like 'Rolls Royce, Rolls Royce, Ford.' The rationale behind Hughes's suggestion was that both the United States and Britain maintained two-ocean navies, while Japan was only deployed in the Pacific. Japan, though, successfully demanded as concessions that the United States promise not to build any new fortifications west of Hawaii, and that Britain not construct any new bases north of Singapore. This provided an ample security buffer around Japan and made it potentially the predominant naval power in the waters off China.

Japan was also reluctant to scrap the *Mutsu*, the world's largest battleship and an object of national pride that had been paid for largely by public subscription. Under the Hughes scheme it would have to be scrapped. A compromise was reached whereby Japan would instead scrap an older ship, which would leave it with two new battleships and an increased tonnage. As a result, the United States would be allowed to complete construction of two new battleships and Britain would be allowed to build two new battleships.

France and Italy were both angered by the suggested ratio assigned to them of 1.7, arguing that the need to maintain large armies during the First World War had necessitated that their naval building plans languish. France demanded, at the very least, the right to have twice as many auxiliary ships as it possessed at present. Hughes had also proposed that the United States and Britain reduce their submarine inventories to a total of 60,000 tons each, and that the other three naval powers would be allowed to maintain their current levels, that is 31,500 tons each for France and Japan, and 21,000 for Italy. France, however, demanded the astonishing total of 90,000 and, as a result, attempts to limit submarines failed. French intransigence caused the ratio to be applied only to capital ships, that is the largest ships, but not to such categories as cruisers, destroyers or submarines. These results were embodied in what became known as the Five Power treaty.

The Five Power treaty, concluded by the United States, Britain, Japan, France, and Italy established the Hughes ratio of 5-5-3-1.7-1.7 for their respective strength in capital ships. Aircraft carriers were not to exceed 27,000 tons each, battleships 35,000 tons, and cruisers 10,000. The maximum calibre of guns to be carried was limited to a maximum of 8 inches for aircraft carriers and cruisers, and 16 inches for battleships. The use of poison gas was also prohibited. As a result of these decisions the United States scrapped 26 ships either already built or under construction, Britain 24, and Japan 16. With a few agreed exceptions a ten-year ban was placed on new naval construction. In a separate treaty these five states agreed to ban the use of poison gas.

The success of the Five Power treaty concluded at Washington has been much debated. It is notable for being the first successful arms control treaty and it did, for a number of years, halt the naval arms race. Britain and the United States at the time welcomed the outcome as enhancing security while removing the spectre of a wasteful armaments race. Some historians have argued, however, that for Britain in the long run it was a disaster, citing for example that the ten-year naval building holiday caused the loss of critical skills and personnel. In this early attempt at arms control there were problems of implementation to overcome. Even in the arms control talks of the 1970s and 1980s verification remained a difficulty. The limitation per ship of a 35,000 ton displacement depended on the honesty of the signatories. Finally, as the treaty only applied to capital ships, it simply shifted naval construction to other categories.

In discussing problems relating to China the parties to the Five Power treaty were joined by another four states with interests there, Belgium, the Netherlands, Portugal and, of course, China. The results would be embodied in the Nine Power treaty. There were fears that China would repeat the role of the Ottoman Empire in becoming the new sick man of the international system and thereby become the cause of potentially dangerous rivalries between competing powers. In the Nine Power treaty the signatories agreed to respect the sovereignty and territorial integrity of China and to maintain the principle of the Open Door, that is an equal opportunity for all states to trade and invest in China. This was no more than an expression of good intentions, without any mechanism for enforcement and little was done when Japan violated its terms when it seized Manchuria in 1931. China was also given greater control of its own customs revenue, which the foreign powers had taken control of to repay debt owed to them, in order to alleviate the Chinese government's severe financial problems.

There were also minor agreements, resolving issues between various parties to the conference, made in the environment of the Washington Conference. Japan agreed to American cable rights on the disputed island of Yap, Japan also agreed to liquidate its military presence in Siberia, no doubt to the relief of both Tokyo and Washington if not the Japanese army; and most importantly, with American and British prodding, Japan agreed to relinquish the Shantung peninsula to China, in return for retaining for a period of years some economic presence. The problem of the Anglo-Japanese alliance was resolved by the Four Power treaty, between Britain, Japan, the United States, and France which terminated the Anglo-Japanese alliance. The signatories agreed to respect each others' existing rights in the Pacific region and to refer future disputes to a joint conference. It was, in essence, a goodwill agreement with a promise to try negotiations rather than force to resolve disputes.

Hughes also attempted to raise the issue of military disarmament. Both the United States and Britain had reduced their armies to prewar levels. The peace treaties already controlled the size of the armies of the former Central Powers, but France had only made a small reduction. France pointed to its continuing concerns about a German threat and the French premier, Briand, argued that moral disarmament, that is a clear disinclination to go to war, would have to precede military disarmament. As a result nothing was achieved in this area.

For Japan what became known as the Washington System marked an important shift in its approach to foreign policy. The dominant figure of Japanese foreign policy during much of the 1920s was its representative at the Washington Conference, Shidehara. He saw in the complex of treaties and agreements negotiated at Washington the basis for a stable East Asian and Pacific international order. With its security safeguarded by general naval arms reduction Japan could now turn to economic concerns. Shidehara's diplomacy saw Japan becoming an increasingly cooperative international actor. Although it succumbed to militaristic elements in the 1930s Shidehara's diplomacy would prove an important intellectual influence in Japanese diplomacy after the Second World War.

At the time the Washington Conference was widely hailed as a significant step towards international stability. The prospect of a financially crippling naval arms race had been prevented, the first substantive arms control treaty had been agreed, the navies of the great powers were to be limited, a clash between the major powers for dominance in east Asia and the Pacific had been avoided, and the Anglo-Japanese alliance that had filled other states with such unease had been replaced by a broader agreement. It would prove to be only a short-term solution. Within ten years the Washington system had collapsed, largely due to the renewed Japanese bid for regional hegemony.

Note

1 Imperial Conference, 2nd meeting, 21 June 1921. Minutes of the Imperial Conference, CAB 32/2, Public Record Office, Kew, London.

CHAPTER EIGHT

LOCARNO

The years that followed the conclusion of the peace treaties with the Central Powers clearly revealed their weaknesses. In particular the unworkability of the financial settlement imposed upon Germany was disrupting not only the stability of Europe but also Euro-American relations. After the vast expenditures of the war, governments were under pressure to cut expenditure and lower taxes. The United States was also insisting on the repayment of loans made by it to the Allies. At the same time the origins of the war came to be scrutinized and many came to the conclusion that the arms races of the prewar period were a contributing factor to the outbreak of war. All these factors led to efforts to reduce armaments, handle debt issues, and tackle the problem of reparations. To accomplish much of this package the rehabilitation of Germany was required, a process that culminated with the Locarno pact.

REPARATIONS AND WAR DEBTS

The Treaty of Versailles had left open the amount of reparations finally to be paid by Germany to the Allied states. A Reparations Commission was established to determine the sum, the method of payment, and to oversee collection and distribution of the reparations. The peace treaty had stipulated that Germany was responsible for losses to civilians and their dependants, the maltreatment of prisoners of war, and the destruction of non-military property. In all, the treaty stipulated ten categories of damages for which reparation was due. Prior to deciding the final sum the Allies met at Spa in July 1920 to agree the percentage each would receive from the expected payments. The Allies proposed their scheme, in January 1921, of a sum rising from 2 billion to 6 billion gold marks a year spread over forty-two years, plus 26 per cent of the value of German exports over this period. In March, Germany responded with an offer of 30 billion gold marks, noting it had already paid 20 billion gold marks in initial payments under the interim provisions of the peace treaty. The Allies, however, estimated

German interim payments at less than half that amount, and ordered that Germany immediately make up the shortfall. When Germany failed to comply the Allies, in March 1921, occupied three cities in the industrially important Ruhr as well as most of the customs posts on Germany's western borders.

In April came the long-awaited report of the Reparations Commission, which concluded that the sum due was 132 billion gold marks. Payment was to be made through the medium of three series of bonds under a complex scheme structured in such a way that it was unlikely that the third series would ever be issued, but which provided leverage against Germany should it prove recalcitrant. The result was that the likely expected payment from Germany would amount to 50 billion gold marks. If Germany did not agree the Allies were prepared to occupy the entire Ruhr. The German government resigned and a new government was formed which accepted the Allied ultimatum at the last moment. The new government included one of the most able officials in Germany, Walther Rathenau, first as Minister of Reconstruction and then Foreign Minister. Rathenau advocated a policy of fulfilment of the Allied impositions as the starting point for rebuilding international relations. As mutual confidence increased there would always be the possibility, through negotiation, to modify the harsher elements of the settlement. At the time this was a policy which made Rathenau a figure of hate to ultra-nationalists, still embittered by the outcome of the war and which, ultimately, led to his assassination in 1922. It would, however, be mirrored very successfully by Gustav Stresemann and culminate in the Locarno Pact and the re-entry of Germany into normal international relations in 1925.

A number of factors combined quickly to undermine the reparations arrangements. Germany was entering a period of dramatic economic chaos, the roots of which lay with the wartime financial policies of the imperial government which had printed more money than it had reserves to back reasonably. As a result, by the end of the war the value of the German mark had fallen by 50 per cent. This fall would accelerate with the upheavals that followed the end of the conflict. As the Allies returned to peacetime economies, the adjustment caused an increase in unemployment and, as a result, a low demand for many potential German exports. This further reduced the hard currency that Germany needed to meet its obligations. Domestically it was now suffering a flight of capital seeking safer homes. By late 1921, the German mark was worth 2 per cent of its prewar value and during 1922 the Allies were forced to agree to a temporary suspension of repayments.

The issue of reparations had become tied up with the more general problems of national war debts. One of the consequences of the First World War was the transition of the United States from a net debtor to a net creditor state. As a result of wartime loans to its Allies, the American government was owed $10.35 billion. In addition, there were debts owed to the private sector. The European allies now argued that Washington should forgive the debt, as the money had mostly been used to purchase war matériel in the United States to fight their common foe. Britain had followed this course at the end of the Napoleonic wars and had benefited from the rapid return of economic stability on the continent. Some argued that general debt cancellation would bring a rapid return to economic stability and prosperity from which all would benefit. Britain itself was owed large sums by France that it could only afford to forgive if its own debt to the United States was wiped out. If this occurred, both Britain and France could afford greater leniency on the issue of German reparations.

The American government, however, adamantly refused all efforts at debt cancellation. It had raised money from its own citizens in the form of Liberty Bonds, which generally paid 4.5 per cent interest. Washington was also able to point out that while the European states claimed an inability to pay they were able to afford expensive armaments programmes. For three years after the war the European states made no moves to repay their debts until, in February 1922, the United States congress acted to have a World War Debt Commission make arrangements for payment.

Britain, anxious to maintain good relations with Washington, negotiated a repayment plan in 1923 under which their debt would be repaid over sixty-two years at 3.3 per cent, a reduction from an original 5 per cent. The reduction reduced the sum owed by almost a third. The other chief debtors, Belgium, France, and Italy proved more recalcitrant, preferring to assure first a stream of reparations payments from Germany. British and French ideas on the debt problem had now diverged. Britain had concluded that it was unlikely that it would ever see much of the German money and began to shift its attention, given its own economic situation, to rehabilitating Germany as a trading partner. Prior to the conflict Germany had been the destination for 25 per cent of Britain's exports. In France a hardline government had been formed under Poincaré in January 1922. He was more interested in keeping Germany weak in the interests of French security. The Reparation Commission consisted of four members, Britain, France, Belgium and Italy. Poincaré was able to sway all the members, except Britain, to support a motion declaring Germany in default. This action provided the justification for France to occupy the Ruhr.

The Ruhr occupation provided the final major crisis in German-Allied relations in the search for a postwar settlement. The Ruhr possessed one of the world's largest coalfields and was one of the greatest industrial regions. After the 1871 war with France, Germany had successfully integrated the iron and steel industries of Lorraine with the coal reserves of the Ruhr. The reacquisition of Lorraine by France at the end of the First World War had not reduced that province's dependence on Ruhr coal, and the Treaty of Versailles provided for the continued purchase of Ruhr coal at preferential prices. Meanwhile the Ruhr's own industries had been badly hit by the loss of iron ore from Lorraine, which had reduced German supplies by 80 per cent. It was the French charge of German failure to deliver adequate supplies of coal which had led to the occupation of three Ruhr towns in 1921. The German population reacted with passive resistance which, while confounding French plans, also acted as the catalyst for an economic meltdown in Germany as a whole.

The Ruhr occupation coincided with, and contributed to, the escalating financial crisis in Germany. Inflation had been growing steadily during the war and now, as pressure on government to meets its many domestic and foreign obligations grew, it increasingly had recourse to the printing press. The result would be one of history's best-known examples of hyper-inflation. At the start of hostilities in 1914 the mark traded against the US dollar at a rate of 4:1, at the end of the war at 9:1, in January 1922 at 191:1, in January 1923 at 18,000:1, and by November 1923 at 4,200,000,000,000 : 1. This hyperinflation impoverished large numbers of Germany's broad middle classes and would be a contributing factor in the polarization of German politics in the years ahead. At the height of the crisis a new chancellor took office who would dominate German politics until his death in 1929 and who was the architect of the rehabilitation of Germany as a full member of the international community. In September 1923 Gustav Stresemann was able to bring an end to the passive resistance in the Ruhr, thereby opening the possibility of reaching some accommodation with the French government led by the hardline premier, Poincaré. He also began measures to stabilize the currency, replacing the old currency with a new *Rentenmark* backed by real assets, cut government spending and balanced the budget. The medicine had been harsh, but 1924 saw a remarkable new stability in German political and economic life.

Stresemann has been seen, in retrospect, as a good European bent on containing militarism and nationalism. The reality is more complex. As a German statesman, guiding German foreign policy, Stresemann was of necessity focused on the immediate issues confronting postwar Germany. He was concerned with issues of German security, financial stability, the restoration of full German sovereignty with the removal of the army of occupation, and the acceptance of Germany as once again an equal state with the other European powers. The burning problem was the occupation of the Ruhr which, in turn, was linked to Germany's default in reparations payments which, in turn, was disrupting the ability of the European allies to repay their wartime debts to the United States.

The United States had opposed the French move against the Ruhr. Despite its non-ratification of the Treaty of Versailles, America had continued to participate in the army of occupation. The Ruhr crisis now led the United States to remove its residual forces from Germany. The American Secretary of State, Charles Evans Hughes, proposed that an international financial commission examine the reparations payments. Britain took the opportunity provided by the ending of the passive resistance to organize such a meeting in London. With renewed American participation it was now possible to pursue a more moderate course. The result was the Dawes Plan, named after the American president of the commission, which opened the way for the evacuation of the Ruhr and the rescheduling of the German debt in a way which adjusted payments to prosperity, and also provided for a loan to Germany to assist its economic recovery. Stephen Schuker, one of the authorities on the financial diplomacy of the period, has concluded that the adoption of the Dawes Plan, 'resulted in an erosion of France's position in Europe that went far beyond the scaling down of German reparations obligations as stipulated in the plan itself. The London Conference of 1924 brought fundamental modification in the economic consequences of the peace; it also undercut the essential military and political supports that upheld the edifice created at Versailles.'[1]

The failure of the French occupation, and the subsequent adoption of the Dawes Plan, mark the end of efforts to use reparations as a method of keeping Germany weak. At the time, although some German nationalists denounced the Dawes Plan as intended to continue the economic enslavement of Germany, the plan in fact opened the way for the economic recovery of Germany. Stresemann's constructive approach to issues of financial diplomacy, and the goodwill this generated, made it possible for Germany to open negotiations on other issues of concern, in particular the weapons inspection regime.

ARMS CONTROL

The year 1899 witnessed the publication of I.S. Bloch's *The Future of War*, in which Bloch argued that technology now made war impossible, as war would be too destructive. The eve of the First World War saw the publication of Norman Angell's *The Great Illusion*, a best seller that argued that war had been made obsolete. The First World War, however, while disproving the impossibility of war, bore out the arguments made in both books about the destructiveness of modern warfare. In Britain the war led to the founding of the Union for Democratic Control (UDC), which was dominated by radical liberals and socialists. As part of their programme for a postwar order they proposed general disarmament. These, or similar views, can be found in the pronouncements of President Wilson. He was concerned about the general level of armaments and was an advocate of arms control. It is, therefore, not surprising to find in his Fourteen Points [*Doc. 3*] a call for a reduction in armaments. After the war this aspiration was embodied in Article 8 of the Covenant of the League of Nations [*Doc. 8*].

As a first step towards assuring international peace the victorious powers sought to disarm Germany and its allies. The Treaty of Versailles was a landmark in disarmament negotiations, being the first time technical advisers assisted in the negotiations and their imprint is to be found in the treaty's detailed limitations on all dimensions of the future German military establishment. The negotiations over the disarmament of the Central Powers would form the basis of arms limitation discussions in years that followed. It also saw the development of a professional group whose careers were mostly spent on arms control and disarmament.

Disarmament of the wartime Central Powers was meant as a prelude to more general disarmament. Aimed initially at eliminating German military power and assuring the security of the victors, this disarmament, it was hoped, would serve as a platform on which to erect a wider arms limitation regime. In their reply to Germany's observations on these terms the Allied and Associated Powers stated that these conditions were intended to serve as the first steps to a general reduction and limitation of armaments. While both the United States and Great Britain significantly reduced their military establishments, France in particular refused to do so, largely out of concern that Germany might not be fully adhering to the limits placed upon its forces.

The problem of verification was, and remains, one of the chief problems in implementing disarmament or arms control agreements. Verification of the Versailles obligations was to be accomplished through Inter-Allied Control Commissions supervising the military, naval, and air clauses. The Versailles treaty obliged Germany to open itself to inspection if deemed necessary by the League Council. The League of Nations body for dealing with such matters was its Permanent Advisory Committee for Military, Naval, and Air Questions. By a resolution on 14 March 1925 commissions of investigation, which were always to be made up of experts of three different nationalities, were given extensive rights of entry and search and full diplomatic immunity and privileges. This, however, was the apogee of attempting a rigorous verification regime.

Germany, under both Weimar and Nazi regimes, sought to escape the restrictions imposed upon it. Verification proved to be difficult to implement. The International Military Control Commission inspectors faced continual lack of cooperation and frequent popular hostility and in 1924 some inspectors were even attacked by a mob. The inspectors' report, sent to the Allied governments in February 1925, provided a list of breaches of Germany's obligations, including the militarization of the police, arms works which had not been converted to other uses, the effective re-establishment of a general staff, and military equipment retained in excess of permitted limits.

Despite the International Military Control Commission's (IMCC) report there is no trace of concern in Allied official circles. This was probably because of a growing belief that Stresemann's, and Germany's, intentions were good. Germany, under Stresemann's guidance, had adopted a policy of cooperation in foreign policy. This conciliatory approach ultimately resulted in Germany's rehabilitation in 1925 after its willing reaffirmation of its acceptance of the borders of western Europe that had been imposed by the Versailles treaty. After this reconciliation the International Military Control Commission was withdrawn from Germany and no further attempts were made to monitor Germany's compliance with the arms control clauses of the treaty.

Efforts were also made at more general agreements on arms control. The interwar period saw two types of approach to arms control, in part because of American non-adhesion to the League of Nations. The first was type-specific, through either bilateral or small group multilateral negotiations, and the second was general comprehensive negotiations intended for universal application. This is a pattern that has continued in varying degrees ever since. The type-specific negotiations began almost immediately while the League of Nations was finding its feet and getting established, and are exemplified by the Washington Naval Conference, which focused on limitations on a particular class of naval vessel. Efforts at general arms control agreements, done for the most part through the League of Nations, enjoyed some success. One example was the 1925 Geneva Protocol, which prohibited the use of poison gas and bacteriological weapons. The drive for arms control continued, with discussions outside the League as well, in part because of United States' non-membership.

COLLECTIVE SECURITY

Article 10 of the League Covenant provided for collective security, but how this was to be provided in practical terms was not clear. The extent of the commitment to provide assistance to a member being attacked by an aggressor state lay at the heart of American rejection of membership. In 1923 the League attempted to find a solution, producing a Draft Treaty of Mutual Assistance. This would have allowed for regional collective security agreements, under the supervision of the League Council. Britain, however, with its geographically widely dispersed empire was not in favour and led the movement for its rejection. The debate over the Draft Treaty, however, helped sour further efforts to find ways to ensure greater stability through addressing the problem of national security. The result was the Geneva

Protocol, which sought to improve the machinery of the League to better cope with the issue. All members would bind themselves to submit disputes to the PCIJ or to arbitration. Refusal to do so or to accept the result would be viewed as an act of aggression. This, at least, would provide objective criteria for determining if a state was an aggressor against which some form of action should be taken. In October 1924 it was unanimously adopted by the League and sent to member governments for signature and ratification. One of the architects of the Protocol was the British prime minister, Ramsay Macdonald. It would be Britain, nonetheless, that would ultimately oversee the demise of the protocol.

In November 1924 Macdonald's Labour government was defeated in a general election and the new, Conservative, government led by Stanley Baldwin, with Austen Chamberlain as foreign secretary, was formed. They did not support the protocol. As with the debate over Article 10 of the Covenant, the government was concerned that it would be forced to apply sanctions when it did not wish to do so. In March 1925 Chamberlain informed the League that Britain would not ratify the Geneva Protocol, thereby killing its chances for adoption. This marks the last serious attempt to strengthen the League by providing mechanisms for collective action. Although the Covenant, agreed to only in 1919, provided for collective action through economic or military sanctions, by 1924 it was clear that several important states were unwilling, in reality, to commit themselves to such actions. Attempts to find ways to assure peace and stability now found their main arena outside the League, through either bilateral or small multilateral negotiations.

THE LOCARNO PACT

The year 1925 dawned in Europe with a palpable atmosphere of fear hanging over the continent, but it would end with a feeling of euphoria that came to be called 'the spirit of Locarno'. The Locarno Pact of 1925 was the result of the convergence of several factors occurring simultaneously between November 1924 and March 1925. First was a renewed German attempt at international rehabilitation through an offer, initially to Britain, of a reguarantee of the western European territorial status quo; second was the desire of France to reinsure its security vis-à-vis Germany through a security pact with Britain; and third was the decision of the new Conservative government in Britain to refuse to ratify the Geneva Protocol.

France remained deeply concerned about the threat that could be posed by a reinvigorated Germany. The German-Soviet Rapallo Treaty of 1922 had dismayed France as it raised an old spectre of a German-Russian alliance. France, as a result of its security concerns, had followed a hardline policy against Germany, that had culminated in the occupation of the Ruhr.

France's interest in fostering a separatist movement in the region was likewise a concern to Germany. In 1922, Germany proposed that the states interested in the Rhine pledge should avoid the use of war for ten years. The hardline French premier, Poincaré, refused. The offer was repeated twice in 1923, with the same result. A number of changes of government in the key European countries during 1924, however, provided an opportunity for a new approach.

In late 1924, a new Conservative government was formed in Britain. The new foreign secretary, Austen Chamberlain, was concerned about the danger to peace inherent in the tense situation on the continent and wanted to find ways to stabilize the situation [*Doc. 17*]. In France, in May 1924, Poincaré's government was defeated in elections and a more moderate government was formed. In April 1925 Briand became foreign minister, with the intent to improve relations with Germany [*Doc. 19*]. This coincided with Stresemann's decision to end the policy of passive resistance in the Ruhr and to embark on a policy of Germany fulfilling its obligations.

Britain was anxious to find a solution that would both meet French concerns about its security while stabilizing the political situation in western Europe. On the suggestion of the British ambassador at Berlin, the German government in January 1925 proposed an international guarantee of the existing borders in western Europe. The situation had been eased by the implementation of the Dawes Plan, which led to France withdrawing most of its troops from the Ruhr in November 1924, with the remnant following in August 1925. Briand, who became foreign minister in April 1925, was interested in exploring the German proposal, as was the Belgian government. A conference was convened at Locarno, attended by delegates from Belgium, Czechoslovakia, France, Germany, Great Britain, Italy and Poland which concluded a set of four treaties, known collectively as the Locarno Pact [*Doc. 18*].

i.   A treaty of mutual guarantee of the Franco-German and the Belgian-German frontiers, with Britain and Italy as guarantors
ii. German-Belgian and German-French arbitration treaties
iii. German-Czechoslovak and German-Polish arbitration treaties
iv. Treaties of mutual assistance in the event of German aggression between France and Poland, and between France and Czechoslovakia

Britain and Italy, as guarantors of the frontier settlement, committed themselves to come to the aid of any one of the parties if another attacked them.

No territorial guarantee was made concerning eastern Europe. France had hoped that its eastern European allies would also receive the benefit of a guarantee, but Britain refused. Issues relating to eastern Europe were of far less concern to Britain than those of western Europe. As a result, France sought to reassure its eastern European allies through the treaties of mutual guarantee signed at Locarno in tandem with the other treaties. Stresemann had probably hoped that Locarno would mark the beginning of displacing the Versailles settlement with a more acceptable one. Some in Germany sought the return of some of the lost colonies, the abrogation of the war guilt clause, and some adjustment to Germany's eastern borders.

Chamberlain, not unaware of the wider concerns of France and Germany, hoped that other 'Locarnos' could be arranged, for example, for eastern Europe and for the Mediterranean, involving the relevant parties. Chamberlain's approach with the negotiations, which culminated with the Locarno Pact, was not to try to cope with too broad a palette of issues but, rather, to keep a tight focus. Once those issues were dealt with it would be possible, in future negotiations, to attempt to deal with others. At the time Locarno was hailed as a great success. Germany had renounced any aspirations to regain Alsace–Lorraine or the remilitarization of the Rhineland. France, in return, had given up acting unilaterally against Germany. Stresemann, of course, had been fully aware that Germany was in no condition to fight a war and was, therefore, only recognizing the reality of the moment. For their work at Locarno Chamberlain, Briand, and Stresemann were awarded the Nobel Peace Prize. The way was now open to the admission of Germany to the League of Nations and, in 1926, it entered the League with a permanent seat on the Council, symbolizing its full rehabilitation and acceptance as a major power.

The British Dominions were concerned that agreements, such at that reached at Locarno, might commit them to involvement in conflicts concerned with European security issues. As a result they were specifically exempted from any obligations under Locarno. By 1925 the bonds of empire can be seen to have been rapidly loosening. The creation of a separate Dominions Office in 1925, far from representing an institutional attempt to tighten imperial connections, was a recognition of the growing divergence of their foreign and defence concerns. Baldwin had unsuccessfully attempted to hold an Imperial Conference to discuss the Geneva Protocol and alternative arrangements, with the Dominions replying that they were too busy to attend. Britain's European concerns were not the Dominions'. In retrospect, this nonchalant response on the part of the Dominions provided the backdrop to the Balfour Report of 1926 and the subsequent Statute of Westminster, which formally cut the dominions free from London and vice versa.

Austen Chamberlain saw Locarno as marking the dividing line between the years of war and the years of peace. After almost seven years of volatility and armed tension the international system at least seemed to have stabilized. Economic issues had been addressed as prosperity was slowly beginning to return. The first steps towards arms control and reduction had been taken. The League of Nations was seen as beginning to establish its role in international relations, and with increasing frequency, the political leaders themselves attended its meeting. Although some disagreed [*Doc. 20*], it was with greater optimism than at any time since 1919 that most people viewed the state of international relations and, for a few years at least, the 'Spirit of Locarno' seemed justified.

Note

1   Stephen Schuker, *The End of French Predominance in Europe: the financial crisis of 1924 and the adoption of the Dawes Plan* (Chapel Hill, NC, 1976), p. 386.

CHAPTER NINE

CONCLUSION

Between the dark devastation surrounding the railway carriage in the clearing in the forest near Compiègne, where the armistice that ended the Great War had been signed, and the clinking of glasses in the glittering room at Locarno in which a new spirit emerged in European relations, a new international order had evolved. The problems unleashed by the First World War, compounded by other issues left unaddressed due to the war, proved more complex than could be resolved at one conference. The actual process of achieving a postwar international settlement stretched over six years, from the Paris Peace Conference of 1919 to the Locarno Conference of 1925. It would be an era of conference diplomacy. This development was in itself a shift from the prewar order. Traditionally, diplomacy had been conducted by the resident ambassadors with the host government, and international conferences were relatively infrequent until after the First World War. Now, taking advantage of improved transport and communications, the political leaders themselves chose to become directly involved in the diplomacy of the day. Whether or not such 'hands-on' negotiating by political leaders is effective, or whether it is best left to intermediaries, is an ongoing debate in the study of diplomacy. Diplomacy by conference, nonetheless, remains one of the hallmarks of the period 1919–25.

The global balance of power was beginning a shift away from the prewar predominance of the great European powers. For the first time the United States and Japan were major participants in international conferences. The French and, in particular, the British empires had been severely weakened by the war. In the case of the British Empire the period 1919–25 saw the critical phase in the reassessment of the relationship between London and the self-governing dominions that would in turn see the dominions set firmly on the road to full independence. This development, together with the introduction of the mandates system, marked the beginning of the end of the age of colonial imperialism and the start of the age of decolonization.

The diplomacy that followed the First World War was able to address many of the immediate issues arising from the conflict. Many problems, however, were contemporary manifestations of much deeper and older concerns. The disintegration of both the Austro-Hungarian and Ottoman empires was the culmination of over a century of events. Both unleashed ethnic tensions that remain enduring problems of international relations. It is difficult to criticize the work of the leaders at that time when subsequent efforts to find solutions have proven equally elusive. Indeed a surprising amount of the settlement reached in the aftermath of the First World War has proved to be remarkably durable and acceptable.

The German problem was central to efforts to construct a stable postwar order. Under the Versailles settlement the German Empire had been greatly pruned. Some of the new boundaries benefited from the legitimization provided through consultation of the inhabitants. Other changes proved more controversial. France throughout this period sought to create some form of hegemony over western Germany. The Locarno Pact finally saw the mutual acceptance of the demarcation arrived at in the Versailles treaty, and which remains the boundary to this day. In the east the problem caused by the physical separation of East Prussia from the rest of Germany would cause ongoing tension with the new Polish state and would remain a sore spot until, as a result of the Second World War, East Prussia ceased to form part of Germany.

A far greater cause of instability proved to be the issue of reparations payments. Economic diplomacy became one of the most important areas of activity after the signing of the Versailles treaty. Previously, foreign ministries had not dealt much with economic issues but, as a result of the series of crises spawned by the reparations provisions, foreign ministries now began to develop structures to grapple with the economic dimensions of foreign policy. The Dawes Plan had provided a solution to the immediate set of crises caused by Germany's inability to meet the high level of repayments that it was expected to meet. In 1929 the Dawes Plan was followed by a further scheme, the Young Plan, which reduced the debt to a quarter of the amount set in 1921 and spread payment over the next 58.5 years. As a result of the Great Depression Germany was unable to make instalments for 1931–32 and, after Hitler took power in 1933, Germany refused to make further payments. The Young Plan replaced the Berlin-based office of the Agent General for reparations with a new Bank for International Settlements, established at Basle, Switzerland in 1929. Also known as the Basle group, the bank remains in existence as the world's oldest international financial institution, providing for cooperation among the world's national central banks.

The effort to identify and try war criminals proved largely abortive. The concept, however, of an international tribunal provided a precedent for the Nuremberg and Tokyo war crimes trials after the Second World War and, later, for the United Nations War Crimes tribunals, and the 1998 Rome Statute proposing an International Criminal Court.

In eastern Europe the turbulent and amorphous political map that had emerged from the war had stabilized by 1925. Much of the energy of these states was engaged in integrating their infrastructure from systems inherited from previous sovereignties. The hope was that the inevitable disputes that would erupt between these states could be resolved by the new international machinery; it was a view that was justified when, in 1925–26, the League of Nations successfully resolved a dispute between Greece and Bulgaria. The minority protection treaties used in this region to facilitate the creation of new, nation-based states, while assuring the rights of ethnic minorities, was an important step in the development of general human rights in the decades that followed.

It was in the area of the evolution of new international bodies that the greatest creativity was to be found during the years in which a new postwar order was emerging. Although the League of Nations would ultimately be seen by many as a failure, through its inability to stop the aggressor states of the 1930s, it provided a valuable lesson in international cooperation. The effectiveness of the ideas embodied in the League is demonstrated through the creation of the United Nations after the Second World War, organized with only small modifications along the lines of the League. The ILO has remained an active body since its inception, while many aspects of the League's work continue under new labels: the Nansen organization as the UN High Commissioner for Refugees, the Committee on Intellectual Cooperation as UNESCO, the Permanent Court of International Justice as the International Court of Justice.

The Russian revolution introduced a new and potent factor into international relations that would be a major concern of the other powers for three quarters of a century. In its earliest and most revolutionary phase the revolutionary government seemed to threaten the existing political orders in all other states. Russian leaders, though, also increasingly turned to the west for essential support in rebuilding the country, and while its rhetoric remained revolutionary Russian diplomacy soon began to follow traditional norms as its government sought to gain international recognition and establish normal diplomatic relations.

The Eastern Question had bedevilled governments for a century before the First World War, it strained relations between the Allies during the peacemaking, the region remained volatile throughout the interwar years and what was known as the Eastern Question remains a flashpoint in international relations. The failure of Greek aspirations and the subsequent refugee crisis caused great tension at the time, but the subsequent settlement reached at Lausanne and the agreement to exchange populations laid the basis for three decades of stability in Greek-Turkish relations. The Middle

East was artificially divided between Britain and France under the guise of League of Nations mandates. This was much more of a patchwork settlement and its unsatisfactory nature has contributed to much of the continuing tensions and instability in the region.

While the conferences held in Europe had done much to address issues of European security, East Asia was possibly one of the most potentially volatile regions of the world after the First World War. Tension was steadily growing between the United States and Japan. Once again resolution was found through the use of conference diplomacy with the Washington Conference addressing the linked issues of East Asian stability and naval rivalry. The solutions arrived at to limit naval armaments would become the starting point in the new field of the study of arms control and arms limitation.

The period of adjustment and peacemaking that followed the First World War finally reached an end with the Locarno Pact in 1925 which readmitted Germany to the international community, an essential step in normalizing international relations. It is sometimes argued that the postwar order was fatally flawed by America's rejection of membership in the League of Nations and the collective security arrangements provided both through its Covenant and those made directly to France in conjunction with Britain. It would be inaccurate, however, to suggest that the United States became isolationist. The Versailles treaty was rejected in 1920 but, by 1921 the American government was already proposing a major international conference at Washington. The United States played an active role in mediating the reparations crisis which lay at the heart of so much of postwar European tension and culminated in the Dawes Plan. While the United States did not adhere to the new Permanent Court of International Justice such figures as former Secretary of State Hughes (who had presided over the Washington conference) served on the bench of this new, international court. If the United States was not the central actor envisaged by Wilson, it remained an active and influential one.

If one individual emerges from the period under consideration it is unquestionably Woodrow Wilson. Controversial both in his lifetime and since, his vision of a world order based on liberal democracy continues to resonate. The world vision of Lenin, since the collapse of the Soviet bloc in 1990–91, now appears transitory. Nonetheless, the rivalry between the competing visions of Wilson and Lenin underlay the critical tension that would dominate international politics in the second half of the twentieth century, during the Cold War. The roles of the other key leaders of the period, however, should not be ignored. Lloyd George was not so distant in his thinking from Wilson, and like the American president was deeply influenced by the British liberal leader Gladstone. Lloyd George brought a less visionary, but more applied, approach to the problems of the period, as shown in his Caxton Hall speech that preceded Wilson's more famous Fourteen Points speech. The French leader, Clemenceau, provides an example of a realist approach. An idealist, it could be argued, in his love for France, he was a realist in his approach to foreign policy. He attempted to identify what was in the French national interest, in this case the long-term weakening of Germany, and then used this as the core of his approach. Each of these leaders was impelled by different pressures and therefore had different priorities. Wilson could look to long-term goals, Lloyd George could afford to consider medium-term objectives, while Clemenceau had to look to the short term. It was not, however, the leaders of the great powers alone during this period who remain memorable. The charismatic Greek premier, Venizelos, who proved one of the greatest diplomatists of the century; the great political survivor in French politics, Briand, who provided a concept of a wider Europe beyond the tensions of nation-centred states, and the pragmatic Stresemann, who rebuilt the standing of a country that had been defeated in the greatest war in history only six years previously simply through effective diplomacy. Perhaps the final mention should be of the vision of the Czech leader, Masaryk, who so aptly saw the postwar world as a laboratory sitting atop a vast cemetery. The twentieth century would indeed continue to see more than its share of violent death and destruction but it would likewise witness some of the most dramatic advances in efforts at stability, most of which emanated from the years 1919–25.

DOCUMENTS

DOCUMENT 1 THE BALFOUR DECLARATION, 2 NOVEMBER 1917

Dear Lord Rothschild,

I have much pleasure in conveying to you, on behalf of His Majesty's Government, the following declaration of sympathy with Jewish Zionist aspirations which has been submitted to, and approved by, the Cabinet.

'His Majesty's Government view with favour the establishment in Palestine of a national home for the Jewish people, and will use their best endeavours to facilitate the achievement of this object, it being clearly understood that nothing shall be done which may prejudice the civil and religious rights of existing non-Jewish communities in Palestine, or the rights and political status enjoyed by Jews in any other country.'

I should be grateful if you would bring this declaration to the knowledge of the Zionist Federation.

Yours sincerely,
Arthur James Balfour

DOCUMENT 2 LLOYD GEORGE'S CAXTON HALL SPEECH, 5 JANUARY 1918

Prime Minister Lloyd George on the British War Aims:

The days of the Treaty of Vienna are long past. We can no longer submit the future of European civilization to the arbitrary decisions of a few negotiators striving to secure by chicanery or persuasion the interests of this or that dynasty or nation. The settlement of the new Europe must be based on such grounds of reason and justice as will give some promise of stability. Therefore, it is that we feel that government with the consent of the governed must be the basis of any territorial settlement in this war. For that reason also, unless treaties be upheld, unless every nation is prepared at whatever sacrifice to honour the national signature, it is obvious that no treaty of peace can be worth the paper on which it is written.

The first requirement, therefore, always put forward by the British Government and their Allies, has been the complete restoration, political, territorial and economic, of the independence of Belgium, and such reparation as can be made for the devastation of its towns and provinces. This is no demand for war indemnity, such as that imposed on France by Germany in 1871. It is not an attempt to shift the cost of warlike operations from one belligerent to another, which may or may not be defensible. It is no more and no less than an insistence that, before there can be any hope for a stable peace, this great breach of the public law of Europe must be repudiated and, so far as possible, repaired. Reparation means recognition. Unless international right is recognized by insistence on payment for injury done in defiance of its canons it can never be a reality.

Next comes the restoration of Serbia, Montenegro and the occupied parts of France, Italy and Roumania. The complete withdrawal of the alien armies and the reparation for injustice done is a fundamental condition of permanent peace.

We mean to stand by the French Democracy to the death in the demand they make for a reconsideration of the great wrong of 1871, when, without any regard to the wishes of the population, two French provinces were torn from the side of France and incorporated in the German Empire. This sore has poisoned the peace of Europe for half a century and, until it is cured, healthy conditions will not have been restored. There can be no better illustration of the folly and wickedness of using a transient military success to violate national right.

I will not attempt to deal with the question of the Russian territories now in German occupation. The Russian policy since the revolution has passed so rapidly through so many phases that it is difficult to speak without some suspension of judgment as to what the situation will be when the final terms of European peace come to be discussed. Russia accepted war with all its horrors because, true to her traditional guardianship of the weaker communities of her race, she stepped in to protect Serbia from a plot against her independence. It is this honourable sacrifice which not merely brought Russia into the war, but France as well. France, true to the conditions of her treaty with Russia, stood by her ally in a quarrel which was not her own. Her chivalrous respect for her treaty led to the wanton invasion of Belgium; and the treaty obligation of Great Britain to that little land brought us into the war.

The present rulers of Russia are now engaged without any reference to the countries whom Russia brought into the war, in separate negotiations with their common enemy. I am indulging in no reproaches; I am merely stating facts with a view to making it clear why Britain cannot be held accountable for decisions taken in her absence and concerning which she has not been consulted or had her aid invoked.

No one who knows Prussia and her designs upon Russia can for a moment doubt her ultimate intention. Whatever phrases she may use to delude Russia, she does not mean to surrender one of the fair provinces or cities of Russia now occupied by her forces. Under one name and another – and the name hardly matters – these Russian provinces will henceforth be in reality part of the dominions of Prussia. They will be ruled by the Prussian sword in the interests of Prussian autocracy, and the rest of the people of Russia will be partly enticed by specious phrases and partly bullied by the threat of continued war against an impotent army into a condition of complete economic and ultimate political enslavement to Germany.

We all deplore the prospect. The democracy of this country means to stand to the last by the democracies of France and Italy and all our other Allies. We shall be proud to fight to the end side by side with the new democracy of Russia, so will America and so will France and Italy. But if the present rulers of Russia take action which is independent of their Allies we have no means of intervening to arrest the catastrophe which is assuredly befalling their country. Russia can only be saved by her own people.

We believe, however, that an independent Poland comprising all those genuinely Polish elements who desire to form part of it, is an urgent necessity for the stability of Western Europe.

Similarly, though we agree with President Wilson that the break-up of Austria–Hungary is no part of our war aims, we feel that unless genuine self-government on true democratic principles is granted to those Austro-Hungarian nationalities who have long desired it, it is impossible to hope for the removal of those causes of unrest in that part of Europe which have so long threatened its general peace.

On the same grounds we regard as vital the satisfaction of the legitimate claims of the Italians for union with those of their own race and tongue. We also mean to press that justice be done to men of Roumanian blood and speech in their legitimate aspirations.

If these conditions are fulfilled Austria–Hungary would become a power whose strength would conduce to the permanent peace and freedom of Europe, instead of being merely an instrument to the pernicious military autocracy of Prussia, which uses the resources of its allies for the furtherance of its own sinister purposes.

Outside Europe, we believe that the same principles should be applied. While we do not challenge the maintenance of the Turkish Empire in the homelands of the Turkish race with its capital at Constantinople, the passage between the Mediterranean and the Black Sea being internationalized and neutralized, Arabia, Armenia, Mesopotamia, Syria and Palestine are in our judgment entitled to a recognition of their separate national conditions. What the exact form of that recognition in each particular case should be need not here be discussed, beyond stating that it would be impossible to restore to their former sovereignty the territories to which I have already referred.

Much has been said about the arrangements we have entered into with our Allies on this and on other subjects. I can only say that as new circumstances, like the Russian collapse and the separate Russian negotiations, have changed the conditions under which those arrangements were made, we are and always have been perfectly ready to discuss them with our Allies.

With regard to the German colonies, I have repeatedly declared that they are held at the disposal of a conference whose decision must have primary regard to the wishes and interests of the native inhabitants of such colonies. None of those territories are inhabited by Europeans. The governing consideration, therefore, in all these cases must be that the inhabitants should be placed under the control of an administration, acceptable to themselves, one of whose main purposes will be to prevent their exploitation for the benefit of European capitalists or governments. The natives live in their various tribal organizations under chiefs and councils who are competent to consult and speak for their tribes and members and thus to represent their wishes and interests in regard to their disposal. The general principle of national self-determination is, therefore, as applicable in their cases as in those of occupied European territories.

The German declaration that the natives of the German colonies have, through their military fidelity in the war, shown their attachment and resolve under all circumstances to remain with Germany is applicable not to the German colonies generally, but only to one of them, and in that case (German East Africa) the German authorities secured the attachment, not of the native population as a whole, which is and remains profoundly anti-German, but only of a small warlike class from whom their Askaris or soldiers were selected. These they attached to themselves by conferring on them a highly privileged position as against the bulk of the native population, which enabled these Askaris to assume a lordly and oppressive superiority over the rest of the natives. By this and other means they secured the attachment of a very small and insignificant minority, whose interests were directly opposed to those of the rest of the population, and for whom they have no right to speak. The German treatment of their native populations in their colonies has been such as amply to justify their fear of submitting the future of those colonies to the wishes of the natives themselves.

Finally, there must be reparation for injuries done in violation of international law. The Peace Conference must not forget our seamen and the services they have rendered to, and the outrages they have suffered for the common cause of freedom.

One omission we notice in the proposal of the Central Powers, which seems to us especially regrettable. It is desirable and, indeed, essential, that the settlement after this war shall be one which does not in itself bear the seed of future war. But that is not enough. However wisely and well we may make territorial and other arrangements, there will still be many subjects of international controversy. Some, indeed, are inevitable.

The economical conditions at the end of the war will be in the highest degree difficult. Owing to the diversion of human effort to warlike pursuits, there must follow a world-shortage of raw materials, which will increase the longer the war lasts, and it is inevitable that those countries which have control of the raw materials will desire to help themselves and their friends first.

Apart from this, whatever settlement is made will be suitable only to the circumstances under which it is made and, as those circumstances change, changes in the settlement will be called for.

So long as the possibility of dispute between nations continues – that is to say, so long as men and women are dominated by passion and ambition, and war is the only means of settling a dispute – all nations must live under the burden, not only of having from time to time to engage in it, but of being compelled to prepare for its possible outbreak. The crushing weight of modern armaments, the increasing evil of compulsory military service, the vast waste of wealth and effort involved in warlike preparation, these are blots on our civilization of which every thinking individual must be ashamed.

For these and other similar reasons, we are confident that a great attempt must be made to establish by some international organization an alternative to war as a means of settling international disputes. After all, war is a relic of barbarism and, just as law has succeeded violence as the means of settling disputes between individuals, so we believe that it is destined ultimately to take the place of war in the settlement of controversies between nations.

If, then, we are asked what we are fighting for, we reply, as we have often replied: we are fighting for a just and lasting peace, and we believe that before permanent peace can be hoped for three conditions must be fulfilled; firstly, the sanctity of treaties must be established; secondly, a territorial settlement must be secured, based on the right of self-determination or the consent of the governed, and, lastly, we must seek by the creation of some international organization to limit the burden of armaments and diminish the probability of war.

On these conditions the British Empire would welcome peace; to secure these conditions its peoples are prepared to make even greater sacrifices than those they have yet endured.

Authorized Version as published by the British Government
New York: George H. Doran Company

DOCUMENT 3 WOODROW WILSON'S FOURTEEN POINTS

(Delivered to a Joint Session of Congress, 8 January 1918)

Gentlemen of the Congress: Once more, as repeatedly before, the spokes-men of the Central Empires have indicated their desire to discuss the objects of the war and the possible basis of a general peace. Parleys have been in progress at Brest-Litovsk between Russian representatives and representatives of the Central Powers to which the attention of all the belligerents have been invited for the purpose of ascertaining whether it may be possible to extend these parleys into a general conference with regard to terms of peace and settlement. The Russian representatives presented not only a perfectly definite statement of the principles upon which they would be willing to conclude peace but also an equally definite program of the concrete application of those principles. The representatives of the Central Powers, on their part, presented an outline of settlement which, if much less definite, seemed susceptible of liberal interpretation until their specific program of practical terms was added. That program proposed no concessions at all either to the sovereignty of Russia or to the preferences of the populations with whose fortunes it dealt, but meant, in a word, that the Central Empires were to keep every foot of territory their armed forces had occupied – every province, every city, every point of vantage – as a permanent addition to their territories and their power. It is a reasonable conjecture that the general principles of settlement which they at first suggested originated with the more liberal statesmen of Germany and Austria, the men who have begun to feel the force of their own people's thought and purpose, while the concrete terms of actual settlement came from the military leaders who have no thought but to keep what they have got. The negotiations have been broken off. The Russian representatives were sincere and in earnest. They cannot entertain such proposals of conquest and domination.

The whole incident is full of significance. It is also full of perplexity. With whom are the Russian representatives dealing? For whom are the representatives of the Central Empires speaking? Are they speaking for the majorities of their respective parliaments or for the minority parties, that military and imperialistic minority which has so far dominated their whole policy and controlled the affairs of Turkey and of the Balkan states which have felt obliged to become their associates in this war? The Russian representatives have insisted, very justly, very wisely, and in the true spirit of modern democracy, that the conferences they have been holding with the Teutonic and Turkish statesmen should be held within open not closed, doors, and all the world has been audience, as was desired. To whom have we been listening, then? To those who speak the spirit and intention of the resolutions of the German Reichstag of the 9th of July last, the spirit and intention of the Liberal leaders and parties of Germany, or to those who resist and defy that spirit and intention and insist upon conquest and subjugation? Or are we listening, in fact, to both, unreconciled and in open and hopeless contradiction? These are very serious and pregnant questions. Upon the answer to them depends the peace of the world. But, whatever the results of the parleys at Brest-Litovsk, whatever the confusions of counsel and of purpose in the utterances of the spokesmen of the Central Empires, they have again attempted to acquaint the world with their objects in the war and have again challenged their adversaries to say what their objects are and what sort of settlement they would deem just and satisfactory. There is no good reason why that challenge should not be responded to, and responded to with the utmost candor. We did not wait for it. Not once, but again and again, we have laid our whole thought and purpose before the world, not in general terms only, but each time with sufficient definition to make it clear what sort of definite terms of settlement must necessarily spring out of them. Within the last week Mr Lloyd George has spoken with admirable candor and in admirable spirit for the people and Government of Great Britain. There is no confusion of counsel among the adversaries of the Central Powers, no uncertainty of principle, no vagueness of detail. The only secrecy of counsel, the only lack of fearless frankness, the only failure to make definite statement of the objects of the war, lies with Germany and her allies. The issues of life and death hang upon these definitions. No statesman who has the least conception of his responsibility ought for a moment to permit himself to continue this tragical and appalling out-pouring of blood and treasure unless he is sure beyond a peradventure that the objects of the vital sacrifice are part and parcel of the very life of Society and that the people for whom he speaks think them right and imperative as he does.

There is, moreover, a voice calling for these definitions of principle and of purpose which is, it seems to me, more thrilling and more compelling than any of the many moving voices with which the troubled air of the world is filled. It is the voice of the Russian people. They are prostrate and all but hopeless, it would seem, before the grim power of Germany, which has hitherto known no relenting and no pity. Their power, apparently, is shattered. And yet their soul is not subservient. They will not yield either in principle or in action. Their conception of what is right, of what is humane and honorable for them to accept, has been stated with a frankness, a largeness of view, a generosity of spirit, and a universal human sympathy which must challenge the admiration of every friend of mankind; and they have refused to compound their ideals or desert others that they themselves may be safe. They call to us to say what it is that we desire, in what, if in anything, our purpose and our spirit differ from theirs; and I believe that the people of the United States would wish me to respond, with utter simplicity and frankness. Whether their present leaders believe it or not, it is our heartfelt desire and hope that some way may be opened whereby we may be privileged to assist the people of Russia to attain their utmost hope of liberty and ordered peace.

It will be our wish and purpose that the processes of peace, when they are begun, shall be absolutely open and that they shall involve and permit henceforth no secret understandings of any kind. The day of conquest and aggrandizement is gone by; so is also the day of secret covenants entered into in the interest of particular governments and likely at some unlooked-for moment to upset the peace of the world. It is this happy fact, now clear to the view of every public man whose thoughts do not still linger in an age that is dead and gone, which makes it possible for every nation whose purposes are consistent with justice and the peace of the world to avow now or at any other time the objects it has in view.

We entered this war because violations of right had occurred which touched us to the quick and made the life of our own people impossible unless they were corrected and the world secure once for all against their recurrence. What we demand in this war, therefore, is nothing peculiar to ourselves. It is that the world be made fit and safe to live in; and particularly that it be made safe for every peace-loving nation which, like our own, wishes to live its own life, determine its own institutions, be assured of justice and fair dealing by the other peoples of the world as against force and selfish aggression. All the peoples of the world are in effect partners in this interest, and for our own part we see very clearly that unless justice be done to others it will not be done to us. The program of the world's peace, therefore, is our program; and that program, the only possible program, as we see it, is this:

I. Open covenants of peace, openly arrived at, after which there shall be no private international understandings of any kind but diplomacy shall proceed always frankly and in the public view.
II. Absolute freedom of navigation upon the seas, outside territorial waters, alike in peace and in war, except as the seas may be closed in whole or in part by international action for the enforcement of international covenants.
III. The removal, so far as possible, of all economic barriers and the establishment of an equality of trade conditions among all the nations consenting to the peace and associating themselves for its maintenance.
IV. Adequate guarantees given and taken that national armaments will be reduced to the lowest point consistent with domestic safety.
V. A free, open-minded, and absolutely impartial adjustment of all colonial claims, based upon a strict observance of the principle that in determining all such questions of sovereignty the interests of the populations concerned must have equal weight with the equitable claims of the government whose title is to be determined.
VI. The evacuation of all Russian territory and such a settlement of all questions affecting Russia as will secure the best and freest cooperation of the other nations of the world in obtaining for her an unhampered and unembarrassed opportunity for the independent determination of her own political development and national policy and assure her of a sincere

welcome into the society of free nations under institutions of her own choosing; and, more than a welcome, assistance also of every kind that she may need and may herself desire. The treatment accorded Russia by her sister nations in the months to come will be the acid test of their good will, of their comprehension of her needs as distinguished from their own interests, and of their intelligent and unselfish sympathy.

VII. Belgium, the whole world will agree, must be evacuated and restored, without any attempt to limit the sovereignty which she enjoys in common with all other free nations. No other single act will serve as this will serve to restore confidence among the nations in the laws which they have themselves set and determined for the government of their relations with one another. Without this healing act the whole structure and validity of international law is forever impaired.

VIII. All French territory should be freed and the invaded portions restored, and the wrong done to France by Prussia in 1871 in the matter of Alsace–Lorraine, which has unsettled the peace of the world for nearly fifty years, should be righted, in order that peace may once more be made secure in the interest of all.

IX. A readjustment of the frontiers of Italy should be effected along clearly recognizable lines of nationality.

X. The peoples of Austria–Hungary, whose place among the nations we wish to see safeguarded and assured, should be accorded the freest opportunity to autonomous development.

XI. Rumania, Serbia, and Montenegro should be evacuated; occupied territories restored; Serbia accorded free and secure access to the sea; and the relations of the several Balkan states to one another determined by friendly counsel along historically established lines of allegiance and nationality; and international guarantees of the political and economic independence and territorial integrity of the several Balkan states should be entered into.

XII. The Turkish portion of the present Ottoman Empire should be assured a secure sovereignty, but the other nationalities which are now under Turkish rule should be assured an undoubted security of life and an absolutely unmolested opportunity of autonomous development, and the Dardanelles should be permanently opened as a free passage to the ships and commerce of all nations under international guarantees.

XIII. An independent Polish state should be erected which should include the territories inhabited by indisputably Polish populations, which should be assured a free and secure access to the sea, and whose political and economic independence and territorial integrity should be guaranteed by international covenant.

XIV. A general association of nations must be formed under specific covenants for the purpose of affording mutual guarantees of political independence and territorial integrity to great and small states alike.

In regard to these essential rectifications of wrong and assertions of right we feel ourselves to be intimate partners of all the governments and peoples associated together against the Imperialists. We cannot be separated in interest or divided in purpose. We stand together until the end.

For such arrangements and covenants we are willing to fight and to continue to fight until they are achieved; but only because we wish the right to prevail and desire a just and stable peace such as can be secured only by removing the chief provocations to war, which this program does remove. We have no jealousy of German greatness, and there is nothing in this program that impairs it. We grudge her no achievement or distinction of learning or of pacific enterprise such as have made her record very bright and very enviable. We do not wish to injure her or to block in any way her legitimate influence or power. We do not wish to fight her either with arms or with hostile arrangements of trade if she is willing to associate herself with us and the other peace-loving nations of the world in covenants of justice and law and fair dealing. We wish her only to accept a place of equality among the peoples of the world – the new world in which we now live – instead of a place of mastery.

Neither do we presume to suggest to her any alteration or modification of her institutions. But it is necessary, we must frankly say, and necessary as a preliminary to any intelligent dealings with her on our part, that we should know whom her spokesmen speak for when they speak to us, whether for the Reichstag majority or for the military party and the men whose creed is imperial domination.

We have spoken now, surely, in terms too concrete to admit of any further doubt or question. An evident principle runs through the whole program I have outlined. It is the principle of justice to all peoples and nationalities, and their right to live on equal terms of liberty and safety with one another, whether they be strong or weak. Unless this principle be made its foundation no part of the structure of international justice can stand. The people of the United States could act upon no other principle; and to the vindication of this principle they are ready to devote their lives, their honor, and everything they possess. The moral climax of this the culminating and final war for human liberty has come, and they are ready to put their own strength, their own highest purpose, their own integrity and devotion to the test.

A. Link, ed., *The Papers of Woodrow Wilson*, vol. 45, *November 11, 1917–January 15, 1918* (Princeton, NJ, 1984), pp. 534–9.

DOCUMENT 4 SONNINO TO SFORZA ON ITALY'S ASPIRATIONS IN THE OTTOMAN EMPIRE, 26 JANUARY 1919

The Italian foreign minister writes here to the under-secretary at the Italian foreign ministry:

Following the entry of America into the war there has been a fundamental change in the international appearance of the interests of the Mediterranean Powers in Asiatic Turkey. Annexations and zones of administration are no longer spoken of; instead assistance to the native peoples, who must be free to choose a great power. To harmonise their aspirations with the principles of Wilson, we can expect France and England at an opportune moment to provoke appeals and petitions from notables, communities, tribes, municipalities and other bodies in favour of their respective help to the regions concerned. True, there exists a strong current amongst the Arabs for absolute independence, but it is likely that this current...will be more or less eliminated....

There may derive from this a danger to Italian aspirations, which are connected with our vital interests in the Mediterranean. Our obvious competitors may oppose our claims, basing themselves on Wilson's principles, by saying that no people in Asiatic Turkey show themselves favourable to Italian assistance, or ask for it. We must see to this.

Sonnino Papers 43/47, reprinted in C. Lowe and F. Marzari,
Italian Foreign Policy, 1870–1940 (London, 1975), p. 394.

DOCUMENT 5 LLOYD GEORGE TO CHURCHILL ON WITHDRAWAL FROM RUSSIA, 16 FEBRUARY 1919

Am very alarmed at your second telegram about planning war against the Bolsheviks. The cabinet have never authorized such a proposal. They have never contemplated anything beyond supplying armies in anti-Bolshevik areas of Russia with necessary equipment to enable them to hold their own, and only in the event of every effort at peaceable solution failing. A military enquiry as to the best methods of giving material assistance to these Russian armies is all to the good, but do not forget that it is an essential part of the enquiry to ascertain the cost. And I also want you to bear in mind that the W.O. reported to the Cabinet that according to their information intervention was driving the anti-Bolshevists parties in Russia into the ranks of the Bolsheviks....If Russia is really anti-Bolshevik, then a supply of equipment would enable it to redeem itself. If Russia is pro-Bolshevik, not merely is it none of our business to interfere with its internal affairs, it would be positively mischievous: it would strengthen and consolidate

Bolshevik opinion. An expensive war of aggression against Russia is a way to strengthen Bolshevism in Russia and create it at home. We cannot afford the burden. Chamberlain [the Chancellor of the Exchequer] says we can hardly make both ends meet on a peace basis, even at the present crushing rate of taxation; and if we are committed to a war against a continent like Russia, it is the road to bankruptcy and Bolshevism in these islands.

The French are not safe guides in this matter. Their opinion is largely biased by the enormous number of small investors who put their money into Russian loans and who now see no prospect of ever recovering it. I urge you therefore not to pay too much heed to their incitements. There is nothing they would like better than to see us pulling the chestnuts out of the fire for them.

I also want you to bear in mind the very grave labour position in this country. Were it known that you had gone over to Paris to propose a plan of war against the Bolsheviks, it would do more to incense organised labour than anything I can think of; and what is still worse, it would throw into the ranks of the extremists a very large number of thinking people who now abhor their methods.

Lloyd George Papers, House of Lords Record Office, F/8/3/19.

DOCUMENT 6 EXCERPT FROM LLOYD GEORGE'S FONTAINEBLEAU MEMORANDUM, 25 MARCH 1919

To achieve redress our terms may be severe, they may be stern and even ruthless, but at the same time they can be so just that the country on which they are imposed will feel in its heart that it has no right to complain. But injustice, arrogance, displayed in the hour of triumph, will never be forgotten or forgiven.

For these reasons I am, therefore, strongly averse to transferring more Germans from German rule to the rule of some other nation that can possibly be helped. I cannot conceive any greater cause of future war than that the German people, who have certainly proved themselves one of the most vigorous and powerful races in the world, should be surrounded by a number of small States, many of them consisting of people who have never previously set up a stable government for themselves, but each of them containing large masses of Germans clamouring for reunion with their native land. The proposal of the Polish Commission that we should place 2,100,000 Germans under the control of a people which is of a different religion and which has never proved its capacity for stable self-government throughout its history must, in my judgment, lead sooner or later to a new war in the East of Europe. What I have said about the Germans is equally true of the Magyars. There will never be peace in South-Eastern Europe if every little state now coming into being is to have a large Magyar Irredenta within its borders. I would therefore take as guiding principle of the peace that as far as is humanly possible the different races should be allocated to their motherlands, and that this human criterion should have precedence over considerations of strategy or economics or communications, which can usually be adjusted. Russia has also given proof that she does not intend to embark upon a military crusade against her neighbours. *It is essential that the leading members of the League of Nations should maintain considerable forces both by land and sea in order to preserve liberty in the world. But if they are to present an united front to the forces both of reaction and revolution, they must arrive at such an agreement in regard to armaments among themselves as would make it impossible for suspicion to arise between the members of the League of Nations in regard to their intentions towards one another. If the League is to do its work for the world it will only be because the members of the League trust it themselves and because there are no apprehensions, rivalries, and jealousies in the matter of armaments between them.* The first condition of success for the League of Nations is, therefore, a firm understanding between the British Empire and the United States of America and France and Italy that there will be no competitive building up of fleets or armies between them. Unless this is arrived at before the Covenant is signed the League of Nations will be a sham and a mockery. It will be regarded, and rightly regarded, as a proof that its principal promoters and patrons repose no confidence in its efficacy. But once the leading members of the League have made it clear that they have reached an understanding which will both secure to the League of Nations the strength which is necessary to enable it to protect its members and which at the same time will make misunderstanding and suspicion with regard to competitive armaments impossible between them its future and its authority will be ensured. It will then be able to ensure as an essential condition of peace that not only Germany, but all the smaller States of Europe undertake to limit their armaments and abolish conscription. If the small nations are permitted to organize and maintain conscript armies running each to hundreds of thousands, boundary wars will be inevitable and all Europe will be drawn in. *Unless we secure this universal limitation we shall achieve neither lasting peace, nor the permanent observance of the limitation of German armaments which we now seek to impose.*

D. Lloyd George, *Memoirs of the Peace Conference* (New Haven, CT, 1939), pp. 266–71.

DOCUMENT 7 CLEMENCEAU AND RELATIONS WITH AMERICA AND GREAT BRITAIN, 2 JUNE 1919

Clemenceau is speaking here in the Council of Four to Lloyd George and Wilson.

My policy at the conference, as I hope you will acknowledge, is one of the close agreement with Great Britain and America. I am not unaware that you have great interests far removed from what most concerns us, I know something of the great American continent and of the immense achievement of the British Empire. Because I have made the entente with England and America the essential foundation of my policy, I am attacked on all sides as weak and incompetent. If I disappeared, you would find yourselves faced with differences even more intractable than those which may separate us today.

There remains the possibility of a final disagreement between us. I don't even want to contemplate it. Let's try to reduce the questions to their narrowest proportions, let's consider only the facts and attempt to see them as they are. If, after that, irreducible points remain between us, I don't know how we will be able to contemplate the future. I don't want to believe that we will have to tell public opinion that we are obliged to break off negotiations because we are incapable of giving a common reply to the Germans.

P. Mantoux, *The Deliberations of the Council of Four* vol. II (Princeton, NJ, 1992), p. 274.

DOCUMENT 8 EXTRACTS FROM THE COVENANT OF THE LEAGUE OF NATIONS

PREAMBLE:
'The high contracting parties, in order to promote international co-operation and to achieve international peace and security by the acceptance of obligations not to resort to war, by the prescription of open, just and honourable relations between nations, by the firm establishment of the understandings of international law as the actual rule of conduct among Governments, and by the maintenance of justice and a scrupulous respect for all treaty obligations in the dealings of organized peoples with one another, agree to this Covenant of the League of Nations.'

ARTICLE 8.1
'The Members of the League recognise that the maintenance of peace requires the reduction of national armaments to the lowest point consistent with national safety and the enforcement by common action of international obligations.'

ARTICLE 10

'The Members of the League undertake to respect and preserve as against external aggression the territorial integrity and existing political independence of all Members of the League. In case of any such aggression or in case of any threat or danger of such aggression the Council shall advise upon the means by which this obligation shall be fulfilled.'

ARTICLE 11

'1. Any war or threat of war, whether immediately affecting any of the Members of the League or not, is hereby declared a matter of concern to the whole League, and the League shall take any action that may be deemed wise and effectual to safeguard the peace of nations. In case any such emergency should arise the Secretary General shall on the request of any Member of the League forthwith summon a meeting of the Council.
2. It is also declared to be the friendly right of each Member of the League to bring to the attention of the Assembly or of the Council any circumstance whatever affecting international relations which threatens to disturb international peace or the good understanding between nations upon which peace depends.'

The Treaty of Versailles and after (Washington, DC, 1947), pp. 72, 82–4.

DOCUMENT 9 ARTICLES 231 AND 232 OF THE TREATY OF VERSAILLES, 28 JUNE 1919

ARTICLE 231

The Allied and Associated Governments affirm and Germany accepts the responsibility of Germany and her allies for causing all the loss and damage to which the Allied and Associated Governments and their nationals have been subjected as a consequence of the war imposed upon them by the aggression of Germany and her allies.

ARTICLE 232

The Allied and Associated Governments recognise that the resources of Germany are not adequate, after taking into account permanent diminutions of such resources which will result from other provisions of the present Treaty, to make complete reparation for all such loss and damage.

The Allied and Associated Governments, however, require, and Germany undertakes, that she will make compensation for all damage done to the civilian population of the Allied and Associated Powers and to their property during the period of the belligerency of each as an Allied or Associated Power against Germany by such aggression by land, by sea and from the air, and in general all damage as defined in Annex 1 hereto.

In accordance with Germany's pledges, already given, as to complete restoration for Belgium, Germany undertakes, in addition to the compensation for damage elsewhere in this Part provided for, as a consequence of the violation of the Treaty of 1839, to make reimbursement of all sums which Belgium has borrowed from the Allied and Associated Governments up to November 11, 1918, together with interest at the rate of five per cent (5%) per annum on such sums. This amount shall be determined by the Reparation Commission, and the German Government undertakes thereupon forthwith to make a special issue of bearer bonds to an equivalent amount payable in marks gold, on May 1, 1926, or, at the option of the German Government, on the 1st of May in any year up to 1926. Subject to the foregoing, the form of such bonds shall be determined by the Reparation Commission. Such bonds shall be handed over to the Reparation Commission, which has authority to take and acknowledge receipt thereof on behalf of Belgium.

The Treaty of Versailles and after (Washington, DC, 1947), pp. 413, 425.

DOCUMENT 10 THE SIGNING OF THE TREATY OF VERSAILLES, 28 JUNE 1919

The following is an extract from the diary of one of the American expert advisers, James Shotwell, describing the signing of the German peace treaty at the palace of Versailles:

The Allied leaders came up the grand staircase through the central aisle of the hall escorted by military attendants to their seats behind the table where the signing was to take place. Then there was a pause and the hall grew absolutely still as the two German delegates were ushered in and given their places at the table, more like men facing sentence at a trial than the representatives of a great Power at an act of sovereignty. They were both deathly pale and nervous, and the nervous tension grew while the Treaty received the signature of the Allied Powers. When finally came the turn of Dr Bell and Herr Müller to sign, one of them found that the pen wouldn't work, and one of Colonel House's secretaries stepped over and pulled his fountain pen from his pocket and handed it to him, and I suppose has the pen as a souvenir still. No sooner had the Germans completed their signatures than immediately, as from some electric signal in the hall, the guns of Saint-Cyr on the southern slopes of Versailles began to boom the announcement to the world outside. Then, fort after fort on the hills around Paris, the heavy guns broke into a salute in a vast reverberating chorus. With a stiff bow, but not exchanging a word of greeting with anyone, the two Germans left the room by the same side door which had admitted them. It seemed to me an added and unnecessary humiliation, but perhaps it saved them from embarrassment.

J. Shotwell, *At the Paris Peace Conference* (New York, 1937), p. 383.

DOCUMENT 11 SIR HORACE RUMBOLD'S ANNUAL REPORT FROM POLAND, 12 MAY 1920

Rumbold was the British minister to the new Polish state, and is here submitting to the Foreign Office the first annual report on Poland:

As Poland principally owes her independence to the sacrifices and efforts made by the Allied and Associated Governments, it is natural that her foreign policy since the armistice should have been based on an intimate association with those Governments. Historical tradition and a certain amount of self-assertion on the part of the French pushed France into the first place amongst the Allies in the estimation of the Polish nation. But as the year 1919 proceeded the position of the French was shaken. Great expectations were founded on America, which had shown itself so generous in the despatch of large sums of relief. When it was realised, however, that the attitude of the American Senate endangered the ratification of the Peace Treaty, Polish public opinion turned from America. Poland then had to consider the only other great Power which counted, and that was Great Britain. However much, therefore, the Polish people and Government may have criticised Great Britain's policy in the Danzig and Eastern Galician questions, they were, and are, well aware that they must reckon with her as their principal ally and adviser.

Situated between two great countries which are for the moment, and will be, possibly for some time to come, powerless for aggression, the Poles had to make up their minds to which of the two Powers they would gravitate in the future. The conclusion was, I think, that the Poles would do the best to look to the East both as an outlet for their trade, and because, being on a higher level of civilisation than the Russians, they will be able to exercise influence on the latter.

The relations between limitrophe States are as often as not the reverse of cordial. As regards their minor neighbours this is true of Poland, whose relations with Lithuania in the North are bad, whilst they are not more than correct with Roumania.

Sir Horace Rumbold to Lord Curzon, 'Poland: Annual Report, 1919', Confidential Print 11549, 12 May 1920, reprinted in *British Documents on Foreign Affairs: Reports and Papers from the Foreign Office Confidential Print*, Part II, Series A, *The Soviet Union, 1917–1939*, vol. 3, *Soviet Russia and Her Neighbours Apr.–Oct. 1920*, D. Watt, ed., 1984, p. 127.

DOCUMENT 12 FORMATION OF THE LITTLE ENTENTE, 14 AUGUST 1920

Convention of Alliance between the Kingdom of the Serbs, Croats, and Slovenes (Yugoslavia) and the Czechoslovak Republic, signed at Belgrade, 14 August 1920.

Firmly resolved to maintain the Peace obtained by so many sacrifices and provided for by the Covenant of the League of Nations, as well as the situation created by the Treaty concluded at Trianon on June 4, 1920, between the Allied and Associated Powers on the one hand, and Hungary on the other, the President of the Czechoslovak Republic and His Majesty the King of the Serbs, Croats, and Slovenes have agreed to conclude a defensive Convention....

Article 1: In case of an unprovoked attack on the part of Hungary against one of the High Contracting Parties, the other Party agrees to assist in the defence of the Party attacked....

A. Keith, *Speeches and Documents on International Affairs, 1918–1937*
(London, 1938), p. 63.

DOCUMENT 13 JAN SMUTS, PRIME MINISTER OF SOUTH AFRICA, ON THE INFLUENCE OF AMERICA ON THE BRITISH EMPIRE, 29 JUNE 1921

Speaking behind closed doors to the Imperial Conference meeting in London Smuts made the following observation:

'If we look to world peace, we must do nothing to alienate Japan or make her think that her time is past, that we have had the convenience of her friendship for twenty years, but that circumstances have changed in the world and we have finished with her; that we are off with the old love and on with the new. I am anxious that we should avoid that, because Japan is the danger of the future; there is no doubt about that. We will not be solving the cause of world peace by shoving her off, so to speak. At the same time I am equally anxious that we should have the right alignment in our foreign policy in the future, and I agree with Mr Meighen [New Zealand prime minister] in what he said this morning, that another generation will see others occupying the position of importance which this Empire occupies to-day. It is quite true to say that America has a vast influence upon the British Empire, and if we want to continue in the future and remain a compact group of States, we have to bear that in mind. We must, in the second place, therefore avoid any policy which might produce a cleavage between ourselves and the United States. We will break up the Empire if we do adopt such a policy. I am quite sure of that, and we must avoid that by all means. One bright spot in this dark situation in which we find ourselves to-day seems to be this, that a Government has come into power in America which wants to work with us. So far we can see from public declarations, the President of America [President Harding] has declared against the League of Nations. He will have nothing to do with that, and he would not join the League of Nations, but there are many indications in the document and in what one sees in the press, that it is really the honest intention of America to work with us, and that America is groping her way towards a closer co-operation with us. Now it is not only this Japanese question that we have to deal with, but with a group of foreign questions. We have some questions with America ourselves, such as Mesopotamia, the question of cables, and so on. Besides that, in the background, there remains the debt which we owe to America, which to my mind it is absolutely necessary to wipe out before we can have good relations restored again. There is going to be a revolt if we continue to build up armaments in this race that is taking place between America and Japan just now. Mr Hughes [Australian prime minister] has just explained to us what they are doing in Australia, and I can see in the economic struggle which is ahead of us in the future that this country is going to be handicapped largely and fatally by the taxation which is necessary for such armaments. Therefore, we have not only the Japanese Alliance, but we have a whole group of first class questions which have to be solved, in the settlement of which America is vitally concerned; and fortunately we have at this juncture an American Administration which appears to want to work with us; and, therefore, I am for dealing with this question as a whole and trying to find a solution, not piecemeal, but of the whole group, if possible. It is quite possible that by a piecemeal solution, by first dealing with the Japanese Alliance and then armaments and other questions, we will get no solution, but with the atmosphere as it is to-day, there ought to be an opportunity and possibility for a solution of the whole group of questions; and I think that we should make use of this opportunity.'

Minutes of the Imperial Conference (10th meeting), 29 June 1921, p. 9.

DOCUMENT 14 SECRETARY OF STATE HUGHES'S SPEECH TO OPENING SESSION OF THE WASHINGTON CONFERENCE, NOVEMBER 1921

We can no longer content ourselves with investigations, with statistics, with reports, with circumlocution of inquiry. The essential facts are sufficiently known. The time has come, and this Conference has been called, not for general resolutions or mutual advice, but for action....

In making the present proposal the United States is most solicitous to deal with the question upon an entirely reasonable and practicable basis, to the end that the just interests of all shall be adequately guarded and that national security and defense shall be maintained. Four general principles have been applied:
(1) That all capital ship-building programs, either actual or projected, should be abandoned;
(2) That further reduction should be made through the scrapping of certain of the older ships;
(3) That in general regard should be had to the existing naval strength of the Powers concerned;
(4) That the capital ship tonnage should be used as the measurement of strength for navies and a proportionate allowance of auxiliary combatant craft prescribed.

The principal features of the proposed agreement are as follows:

CAPITAL SHIPS

United States:

The United States is now completing its program of 1916 calling for 10 new battleships and 6 battle cruisers. One battleship has been completed. The others are in various stages of construction; in some cases from 60 to over 80 per cent of the construction has been done. On these 15 capital ships now being built over $330,000,000 have been spent. Still, the United States is willing in the interest of an immediate limitation of naval armament to scrap all these ships.

The United States proposes, if this plan is accepted:
(1) To scrap all capital ships now under construction. This includes 6 battle cruisers and 7 battleships on the ways and in course of building, and 2 battleships launched. The total number of new capital ships thus to be scrapped is 15. The total tonnage of the new capital ships when completed would be 618,000 tons.

(2) To scrap all of the older battleships up to, but not including, the *Delaware* and *North Dakota*. The number of those battleships to be scrapped is 15. Their total tonnage is 227,740.

Thus the number of capital ships to be scrapped by the United States, if this plan is accepted, is 30, with an aggregate tonnage (including that of ships in construction, if completed) of 845,740 tons.

Great Britain:

The plan contemplates that Great Britain and Japan shall take action which is fairly commensurate with this action on the part of the United States.

It is proposed that Great Britain:

(1) Shall stop further construction of the 4 new *Hoods*, the new capital ships not laid down but upon which money has been spent. These 4 ships, if completed, would have tonnage displacement of 172,000 tons.

(2) Shall, in addition, scrap her pre-*Dreadnoughts*, second line battleships, and first line battleships up to, but not including, the *King George V* class. These, with certain pre-*Dreadnoughts* which it is understood have already been scrapped, would amount to 19 capital ships and a tonnage reduction of 411,375 tons.

The total tonnage of ships thus to be scrapped by Great Britain (including the tonnage of the 4 *Hoods*, if completed) would be 583,375 tons.

Japan:

It is proposed that Japan:

(1) Shall abandon her program of ships not yet laid down, viz the *Kii*, *Owari*, *No. 7* and *No. 8* battleships, and *Nos 5, 6, 7*, and *8*, battle cruisers.

It should be observed that this does not involve the stopping of construction, as the construction of none of these ships has been begun.

(2) Shall scrap 3 capital ships (the *Mutsu* launched, the *Tosa*, and *Kago*, in course of building) and 4 battle cruisers (the *Amgai* and *Akagi* in course of building, and the *Atoga* and *Takao* not yet laid down, but for which certain material has been assembled).

The total number of new capital ships to be scrapped under this paragraph is 7. The total tonnage of these new capital ships when completed would be 289,100 tons.

(3) Shall scrap all pre-*Dreadnoughts* and battleships of the second line. This would include the scrapping of all ships up to but not including the *Settsu;* that is, the scrapping of 10 older ships, with a total tonnage of 159,828 tons.

The total reduction of tonnage on vessels existing, laid down, or for which material has been assembled (taking the tonnage of the new ships when completed), would be 448,928 tons.

Thus, under this plan there would be immediately destroyed, of the navies of the three Powers, 66 capital fighting ships, built and building, with a total tonnage of 1,878,043.

It is proposed that it should be agreed by the United States, Great Britain, and Japan that their navies, with respect to capital ships, within three months after the making of the agreement shall consist of certain ships designated in the proposal and numbering for the United States 18, Great Britain 22, for Japan 10.

The tonnage of these ships would be as follows: of the United States, 500,650; of Great Britain, 604,450; of Japan, 299,700. In reaching this result, the age factor in the case of the respective navies has received appropriate consideration.

> C. Hughes, *The Pathway of Peace: Representative Address Delivered During His Term as Secretary of State (1921–1925)* (New York, 1925), pp. 25–30.

DOCUMENT 15 DEMISE OF THE TREATY OF SÈVRES, 1923

Soon after the Paris Peace Conference ended it was decided to write an immediate history, and this multi-volume history became the first major study of the postwar settlement, written largely by scholars who had worked at the conference. Here the unravelling of the Turkish settlement is described:

By mid-June 1923...Penelope's web had been unravelled almost to the last threads, and the rougher fabric woven out of the torn and tangled materials progressively discarded from the first design was on the verge of completion. Long before the Treaty of Lausanne was signed, however, the Treaty of Sèvres had become an historical curiosity....A treaty thus conceived was doomed from the outset to failure, but the impossible experiment need never have been attempted, and in that case the relations between the victorious Western Powers and the Near and Middle Eastern peoples after the Armistice of 1918 would undoubtedly have taken a very different course from that which they actually followed. From this point of view, the attempt and the error embodied in the abortive diplomatic instrument exercised an enduring influence upon international affairs, and students of its after-effects might, for many years to come, turn back with interest to a 'scrap of paper' which had stimulated such practical and effective opposition.

> H. Temperley, *A History of the Peace Conference of Paris*, vol. VI, (London, 1924), pp 104–5.

DOCUMENT 16 EXCERPT FROM TREATY OF ALLIANCE AND FRIENDSHIP BETWEEN FRANCE AND CZECHOSLOVAKIA, 25 JANUARY 1924

Article 1: The Governments of the French Republic and of the Czechoslovak Republic undertake to concert their action in all matters of foreign policy which may threaten their security or which may tend to subvert the situation created by the Treaties of Peace of which both parties are signatories.

Article 2: The High Contracting Parties shall agree together as to the measures to be adopted to safeguard their common interests in case the latter are threatened.

Article 5: The High Contracting Parties solemnly declare that they are in complete agreement as to the necessity, for the maintenance of peace, of taking common action in the event of any attempt to restore the Hohenzollern dynasty in Germany and they undertake to consult each other in such a contingency.

A. Keith, ed., *Speeches and Documents on International Affairs, 1918–1937* (London, 1938).

DOCUMENT 17 AUSTEN CHAMBERLAIN (BRITISH FOREIGN SECRETARY) TO LEOPOLD AMERY, 19 JUNE 1925

Discussing the Locarno Pact and European security:

'All our history shows that the Channel and the Channel ports have a vital interest for us. Nay, more. It shows how difficult it is for a country situated within twenty miles of the coast of the Continent of Europe to remain untouched by any great conflict that breaks out there. It is not unlikely that if the position of the British Empire had been clearly defined in the early months of 1914 we might have escaped war. It is certain that the first result of American abstention and of the lapse of the Anglo-American pact was the alliances between France on the one hand and Poland and Czecho-Slovakia on the other, and the assumption by France of obligations and relations which are now one of the great complications of the present situation. If we withdraw from Europe I say without hesitation that the chance of permanent peace is gone and that the world must make up its mind that that [*sic*] sooner or later – perhaps in a couple of generation – a new disaster will fall upon us and civilisation itself may perish.'

Austen Chamberlain Papers, University of Birmingham, AC52/38.

DOCUMENT 18 EXCERPT FROM THE LOCARNO PACT, 16 OCTOBER 1925

Signed by Germany, Belgium, France, and Great Britain:

Article 1: The High Contracting Parties collectively and severally guarantee, in the manner provided in the following Articles, the maintenance of the territorial *status quo* resulting from the frontiers between Germany and Belgium and between Germany and France, and the inviolability of the said frontiers as fixed by or in pursuance of the Treaty of Peace signed at Versailles on June 28, 1919....

The Treaty of Versailles and after (Washington, DC, 1947), p. 842.

DOCUMENT 19 BRIAND ON THE ORIGIN AND JUSTIFICATION OF LOCARNO, 25 FEBRUARY 1926

Briand made the following comments before the French Chamber of Deputies:

'What struck me at the time of the discussion of the Treaty of Versailles, which I mentioned at the Commission of Foreign Affairs and must repeat to you now, was the tragic dialogue which was carried on between different members of the Chamber at that time, over the pressing concern to guarantee the security of France.

This was indeed the thought which dominated the whole assembly. The material conditions of the Treaty, although they were important, were of a secondary consideration. We were emerging from a hideous war, and we had only one idea: to avoid another war, and the whole discussion centred on this point. This was the dialogue I heard:

Are we certain that the clause of the Treaty in which we renounce the guarantee of a natural frontier, the clause which promises us the combined guarantee of the USA and Britain, will work? Certain indications from the USA, certain disturbing political facts which could give rise to the thought that the treaty would not be ratified, were set forth as a justification for these doubts.

The honourable president of the Council at that time [Clemenceau], whom you could not reproach with not being concerned with his country's security, said, "I hope that the USA will ratify the Treaty."

When one speaker added, "But if the treaty is not ratified by the USA, what will become of the British guarantee?," M. Clemenceau replied, "I hope that the British guarantee will work."

When someone insisted again, saying, "This British guarantee is bound up with the American guarantee; it is an integral part of it, and if the latter country fails, and Britain consequently considers herself free, what will happen then?", I can still see M. Clemenceau raising his hands and murmuring, "Well, then, there will no longer be a Treaty; there will be nothing."

Well! Gentlemen, when chance circumstances brought me to power in 1921, I considered that my first duty was to use all my strength, all my mind and all my heart, to try to fill in this gap....

At the Cannes Conference, and even before that conference, discussions were undertaken and continued on this subject with representatives of the British government. Their outcome was favourable....It was agreed that the British guarantee would be given. The text of the proposal for the agreement was published.

At the same time, gentlemen, the notion of the Geneva protocol was born in Cannes. There the whole organization of the Genoa Conference for the whole of Europe was being prepared, in which no nation could participate without previously signing a non-aggression pact. Hence we thought that we could bring to the nations of Europe a whole vast system of peace, a whole vast plan of international organization.

Was it a matter of an ordinary alliance, similar to all the others between Britain and France? No, gentlemen! And you will find in the Blue Book, which the British government published at the time, a record of discussions during which it had been perfectly understood that, when a guarantee agreement had been made between Britain and France, Germany could, and even must, enter.

Gentlemen, this is the very essence of the Locarno Treaty. When the worthy M. Herriot had the reparations plan with which you are acquainted accepted in London, the question of an understanding between the peoples of Europe was naturally again put forward to carry out this plan.

It was then that the suggestion of Mr Stresemann, that is, the suggestion of the German government, originated. I seized upon this suggestion. In it I found again the thought that I had had at Cannes. I considered that the events which had taken place since 1921 were such as to strengthen in my mind the wish to form a new agreement whose necessity had become apparent to me, and I gave this my greatest attention.'

J. Néré, *The Foreign Policy of France from 1914 to 1945* (London, 1975), pp. 283–4.

DOCUMENT 20 CLEMENCEAU ON THE POSTWAR SETTLEMENT

Georges Clemenceau, in retirement, remained a fierce critic of what he saw as the disastrous dismantling of the security system established by the Versailles treaty:

'I call a retrograde a peace by which the victor, through whatever short-comings, surrenders to the vanquished part of the advantages purchased with blood upon the battlefields. Whether they be due to weakness of mind or faintness of heart, flaws of character are as much to be dreaded in peace as in war, since they lead a man just as inevitably to surrender his dignity, his will, his personality, everything that constitutes his worth in the widely differing circumstances of peace and war....When I am told that a policy of concessions, more or less happily graduated, is going to regain for us the goodwill of our former enemies I can only be glad to hear it, for I desire nothing so much as a state of stable equilibrium in Europe. But I must be able to perceive some sign of a favourable response to the goodwill that I am asked to manifest. Judge then of my surprise when I discover that *Germany goes on arming and France disarming.* The position is that the most scientific preparations for war are being carried out on the other side of the frontier. With us frontiers lie open, armaments are insufficient, effectives are well below the numbers recognized as necessary, while on the other side a feverish life of reconstruction is developing and reorganizing, by the adaptation of fresh matériel, every department of their war equipment as well as their means of transport. Never was work more generally agreed upon. No complaining. No resistance. Goodwill. Universal enthusiasm the moment that the word "war" is thrown to the passions of the mob, and no sign of a Franco-German reconciliation.'

Georges Clemenceau, *Grandeur and Misery of Victory* (London, 1930), pp. 355, 366–7.

WHO'S WHO

Abdullah (1882–1951) Amir of Transjordan, 1921–46, King of Jordan, 1946–51. Second son of Sharif Hussein of Mecca and brother of Faisal, King of Iraq.

Atatürk, see Kemal, Mustapha

Beneš, Eduard (1884–1948) Czechoslovak foreign minister, 1925–32, and later president.

Borah, William (1865–1940) United States Senator (Republican) from Idaho, 1907–40; chairman, Senate Foreign Relations Committee, 1924–33. Isolationist, supported disarmament conference, 1921–22.

Bourgeois, Léon (1851–1925) Author of the French plan for the creation of a League of Nations.

Briand, Aristide (1862–1932) French premier 1909–11, 1913–17, 1921–22, 1925–26, 1929, 1932; foreign minister, 1925–32. Nobel Peace Prize (1926).

Bukharin, Nikolay Ivanovich (1888–1938) Russian communist leader, member of Politburo, 1924–29; head of Comintern, 1926–29. Executed, 1938.

Cecil, Lord Robert (1864–1958) British member of Parliament (Conservative), 1906–23; Minister of Blockade, 1916–18; Assistant Secretary of State for Foreign Affairs, 1918–19; President, League of Nations Union, 1923–45. One of the drafters of the League of Nations covenant.

Chamberlain, Austen (1863–1937) British Chancellor of the Exchequer, 1903–05, 1919–21; Conservative party leader, 1921–22; Foreign Secretary, 1924–29. Nobel Peace Prize (1925).

Chiang Kai-shek [Jiang Jeishi] (1887–1975) Chinese Nationalist leader. Joined revolutionary government at Canton, 1918, and developed its army.

Churchill, Winston (1874–1965) British Minister of Munitions, 1917–19; Secretary of State for War and Air, 1919–21; Colonial Secretary, 1921–27; Chancellor of the Exchequer, 1924–29. Later Prime Minister.

Clemenceau, Georges (1841–1929) French premier 1906–09, 1917–20; headed French delegation at Paris Peace Conference, 1919.

Crowe, Sir Eyre (1864–1925) British Foreign Office official; permanent under-secretary of state for foreign affairs, 1920–25.

Curzon, George (1859–1925) British Foreign Secretary, 1919–24; represented Britain at the Lausanne Conference, 1923; Lord President of the Council, 1924–25. Created Marquess, 1921.

D'Annunzio, Gabriele (1863–1938) Italian author and politician. Seized Fiume, 1919–20, and ruled it as dictator in defiance of the Allies until deposed by Italy.

Dawes, Charles (1865–1951) United States statesman and financier; head of commission which drew up the 'Dawes Plan' rescheduling Germany's reparations payments (1924); Nobel Peace Prize (1925); US vice president, 1925–29.

Denikin, Anton Ivanovich (1872–1947) Russian soldier; led White army in the south, 1918–20; fled, 1920.

Drummond, Sir Eric (1876–1951) British diplomat and international administrator; founding Secretary-General of the League of Nations, 1919–33.

Faisal (1885–1933) King of Syria, 1920; deposed by France, 1920; King of Iraq, 1921–33. Third son of Sharif Hussein of Mecca and brother of Abdullah, Amir of Transjordan.

Geddes, Sir Eric (1875–1937) Member, British War Cabinet, 1919, Minister of Transport, 1919–21; author of the public expenditure reduction scheme the 'Geddes Axe', 1922.

Gompers, Samuel (1850–1924) United States labour leader; founder of the American Federation of Labor, 1886.

Harding, Warren (1865–1923) President of the United States (Republican), 1921–23.

Hoover, Herbert (1874–1965) United States Food Administrator, 1917–19; Secretary of Commerce, 1921–29; President (Republican), 1929–33.

Horthy, Miklós (1868–1957) Austro-Hungarian admiral and later regent of Hungary, 1919–44.

Hughes, Charles Evans (1862–1948) United States Secretary of State, 1921–25; Judge of the Permanent Court of International Justice, 1928–30; Chief Justice of the United States Supreme Court, 1930–41.

Hughes, William (Billy) (1862–1948) Australian Prime Minister, 1915–23; and Minister for External Affairs, 1921–23.

Hussein ibn 'Ali (c. 1854–1931) Leader of the Arab National Revolt against the Ottoman Empire. Amir of Mecca, 1908–16, King of the Hejaz, 1916–24.

Ishii, Kikujirô (Viscount) (1866–1945) Japanese foreign minister, 1914–16; negotiated Lansing–Ishii agreement, 1917; ambassador to France, 1920–27.

Jiang Jeishi, see Chiang Kai-shek.

Károlyi, Count Mihály (1875–1955) Hungarian statesman; premier, 1918; proclaimed a Hungarian republic, 16 November 1918; president, 1919.

Kemal, Mustapha [later surnamed Atatürk] (1881–1938) Ottoman general; founder of the Republic of Turkey; president, 1923–38.

Keynes, John Maynard (1883–1946) British economist; principal British Treasury representative at Paris Peace Conference, 1919. Resigned in disagreement with policy, 1919.

Kolchak, Alexander Vasilevich (1874–1920) Russian admiral; war minister in the anti-Bolshevik government at Omsk, 1918; supreme leader, 1918–19. Executed by the Bolsheviks, 1920.

Koo, Wellington (1888–1985) Member of Chinese delegation to the Paris Peace Conference, 1919; to the Washington Conference, 1921–22; foreign minister, 1922–24.

Kun, Béla (1868–1939) Founder of the Hungarian communist party, leader of the Hungarian Communist Party (1919). Executed by Stalin.

Lansing, Robert (1864–1928) United States Secretary of State, 1915–20.

Lenin, Vladimir Ilyich (1870–1924) Leader of the Bolshevik faction of the Russian communist movement, Soviet premier, 1917–24.

Lloyd George, David (1863–1945) British statesman; elected to the British Parliament, 1890; entered the cabinet, 1905; Chancellor of the Exchequer, 1908–15; Prime Minister, 1916–22.

Lodge, Henry Cabot (1850–1924) United States Senator (Republican) from Massachusetts, 1893–1924; chairman, Senate Foreign Relations Committee, 1919–24.

Makino, Nobuaki (1861–1949) Japanese diplomat; represented Japan at Paris Peace Conference, 1919.

Masaryk, Tómaš (1850–1937) President of Czechoslovakia, 1918–35.

Nansen, Fritjof (1861–1930) Norwegian explorer and statesman; League of Nations High Commissioner for Refugees, 1921–30. Nobel Peace Prize (1922).

Nitti, Francesco (1868–1953) Italian minister of finance, 1917–19; premier, 1919–20.

Orlando, Vittorio (1860–1952) Italian premier, 1917–19; led Italian delegation to Paris Peace Conference, 1919.

Philimore, Walter (1845–1929) British jurist; chairman British government committee on a League of Nations, 1917–18. Created baron, 1918.

Pilsudski, Józef (1867–1935) Polish head of state, 1918–22; and chief of staff of army, 1918–27.

Poincaré, Raymond (1860–1934) French statesman; elected deputy, 1887; senator, 1906–13; premier, 1912–13; president 1913–20; premier, 1922–24, 1926–29.

Rathenau, Walther (1867–1922) German minister of reconstruction, 1921; foreign minister, 1922. Assassinated, 1922.

Renner, Karl (1870–1950) Austrian chancellor, 1918–19, 1919–20; foreign minister, 1920.

Saionji, Kimmochi (1849–1940) Japanese elder statesman (*genrô*); represented Japan at the Paris Peace Conference, 1919. Created prince, 1922.

Sazonov, Serge Dmitrievich (1861–1927) Russian statesman, minister of foreign affairs, 1910–16; foreign minister in Kolchak's anti-Bolshevik government.

Shidehara Kijûrô (1872–1951) Japanese ambassador to the United States, 1919–22; foreign minister, 1924–27, 1929–31; prime minister, 1945–46.

Smuts, Jan (1870–1950) South African statesman, member of the British War Cabinet (1917–19), attended the Paris Peace Conference, 1919; prime minister of South Africa, 1919–24, 1939–48.

Stresemann, Gustav (1878–1929) German politician; chancellor, 1923; foreign minister, 1923–29. Nobel Peace Prize (1926).

Thomas, Albert (1878–1932) French socialist politician, first director-general of the International Labour Organization.

Trotsky, Leon (1879–1940) Soviet commissar for foreign affairs, 1917–18; commissar for war, 1918–24; creator of the Red Army.

Venizelos, Eleutherios (1864–1936) Greek statesman; premier, 1917–20, 1924; represented Greece at the Paris Peace Conference, 1919, and the Lausanne Conference, 1923.

Wilson, Woodrow (1856–1924) President of the United States, 1913–21. Suffered incapacitating stroke, September 1919. Nobel Peace Prize (1919).

Zinoviev, Grigory Yevseyevich (1883–1936) Chairman of external committee of the Comintern, 1919–26. Executed, 1936.

GUIDE TO FURTHER READING

AUTOBIOGRAPHIES, MEMOIRS, DIARIES AND BIOGRAPHIES

Major political leaders

G. Clemenceau, *Grandeur and Misery of Victory* (London, 1930); D. Lloyd George, *Memoirs of the Peace Conference* (New Haven, CT, 1938), 2 vols; J. Nordholt, *Woodrow Wilson: a life for world peace* (Berkeley, CA, 1991).

Other statesmen

R. Mackay, *Balfour: Intellectual Statesman* (Oxford, 1985); J. Tomes, *Balfour and Foreign Policy: the international thought of a Conservative statesman* (Cambridge, 1997); H. Nicolson, *Curzon: the last phase, 1919–25* (London, 1937) is a classic; also D. Gilmour, *Curzon* (London, 1994).

THE PARIS PEACE CONFERENCE AND THE TREATY OF
VERSAILLES

Collections of documents

The most comprehensive collection of primary documents are *Documents on British Foreign Policy, 1919–1939*, First Series (London, 1947–67); *British Documents on Foreign Affairs: Reports and Papers from the Foreign Office Confidential Print*, K. Bourne and D. Watt, eds, Part II, Series I, *The Paris Peace Conference of 1919*, M. Dockrill, ed., 1989; *Papers Relating to the Foreign Relations of the United States: The Paris Peace Conference, 1919*, 13 vols (Washington, DC, 1942–47); and A. Link, ed., *The Papers of Woodrow Wilson* vols 86–92, (Princeton, NJ, 1986–92); A. Luckau, *The German Delegation at the Paris Peace Conference* (New York, 1940).

General books

M. Dockrill and J. Goold, *Peace without Promise: Britain and the Peace Conferences, 1919–23* (London, 1981); A. Sharp, *The Versailles Settlement: Peacemaking in Paris, 1919* (Basingstoke, 1991). The classic contemporary history, written by participants immediately after the Paris Peace Conference is H. Temperley, ed., *A History of the Peace Conference of Paris* (London, 1920–24), 6 vols; a lively account is provided in W. Churchill, *The World Crisis: The Aftermath* (London, 1929); the most comprehensive recent account is the collections of essays in M. Boemke, *et al.*, *The Treaty of Versailles: a reassessment after 75 years* (Cambridge, 1998) and M. Dockrill and J. Fisher, *The Paris Peace Conference 1919: peace without victory?* (New York, 2001).

Historiography

M. Trachtenberg, 'Versailles after Sixty Years', *Journal of Contemporary History* 17 (1982): 487–506. Earlier works also help illustrate the evolution of work in this subject, R. Binkley, 'Ten Years of Peace Conference History', *Journal of Modern History* 1 (1929): 607–29; R. Binkley, 'New Light on the Paris Peace Conference', *Political Science Quarterly* 46 (1931): 335–61, 509–47 and P. Birdsall, *Versailles Twenty Years After* (New York, 1941); G. Martel, 'The Prehistory of Appeasement: Headlam–Morley, the Peace Settlement and Revisionism', *Diplomacy & Statecraft* 9:3 (1999): 242–65.

On the emergence of conference diplomacy, by one of its creators see M. Hankey, *Conference Diplomacy* (London, 1946).

Studies of the major participants

D. Watson, *Clemenceau: a political biography* (London, 1974); on Lloyd George an insightful account is A. Lentin, 'Several Types of Ambiguity: Lloyd George at the Paris Peace Conference', *Diplomacy & Statecraft* 6 (1995): 223–51; on Woodrow Wilson see L. Ambrosius, *Woodrow Wilson and the American Diplomatic Tradition: the treaty fight in perspective* (Cambridge, 1987).

Probably the best known and most readable memoir of the Paris Peace Conference is H. Nicolson, *Peacemaking 1919* (London, 1933); for a sense of feelings in the junior ranks of the American delegation see C. Seymour, *Letters from the Paris Peace Conference* (New Haven, CT, 1965).

The period leading up to the peace conference

A. Walworth, *America's Moment, 1918: American Diplomacy at the end of World War I* (New York, 1977); B. Lowry, *Armistice 1918* (Kent, OH, 1996).

The plans and aspirations of the great powers can be found in the following, for France D. Stevenson, *French War Aims Against Germany, 1914–1919* (Oxford, 1982); for Britain, E. Goldstein, *Winning the Peace: British Diplomatic Strategy, Peace Planning, and the Paris Peace Conference, 1916–1920* (Oxford, 1991); M. Dockrill, 'The British Empire and the Peace Conferences, 1919–23', *Historian* 42 (1994): 3–8; for the United States L. Gelfand, *The Inquiry: American Preparations for Peace, 1917–1919* (New Haven, CT, 1963) and A. Walworth, *Wilson and His Peacemakers: American diplomacy at the Paris Peace Conference, 1919* (New York, 1986); and for Italy R. Albrecht-Carrie, *Italy at the Paris Peace Conference* (New York, 1938). The nature of the historic Anglo-French rivalry is discussed in 'Britain and Europe', *Diplomacy & Statecraft*, vol. 8, no.3 (1997): 1–177. The activities of the smaller states are dealt with in S. Bonsal, *Suitors and Supplicants* (New York, 1946).

On the Rhineland see R. McCrum, 'French Rhineland Policy at the Peace Conference, 1919', *Historical Journal* 21 (1978): 623–48; W. MacDougall, *France's Rhineland Diplomacy, 1914–1924: the last bid for a balance of power in Europe* (Princeton, NJ, 1978); J. Gerard, *Bridge on the Rhine: American Diplomacy and the Rhineland, 1919–1923* (Ann Arbor, MI, 1977).

Other territorial issues

S. Marks, *Innocent Abroad: Belgium at the Paris Peace Conference of 1919* (Chapel Hill, NC, 1981); R. Johansson, *Small State in Boundary Conflict: Belgium and the Belgian-German Border, 1914–1919* (Lund, 1988); N. Petsalis-Diomidis, *Greece at the Paris Peace Conference 1919* (Thessaloniki, 1978); K. Lundgreen-Nielsen, *The Polish Problem at the Paris Peace Conference: a study of the policies of the great powers and the Poles, 1918–1919* (Odense, 1979); F. Campbell, 'The Struggle for Upper Silesia, 1919–1922', *Journal of Modern History* 42 (1970): 361–85; A. Cienciala, 'The Battle of Danzig and the Polish Corridor at the Paris Peace Conference of 1919', in P. Latawski, ed., *The Reconstrucion of Poland, 1914–1923* (London, 1992); E. Goldstein, 'New Diplomacy and the New Europe at the Paris Peace Conference of 1919: The A.W.A. Leeper Papers', *East European Quarterly* 21:4 (1988): 393–400. S. Spector, *Rumania at the Paris Peace Conference* (New York, 1962); I. Lederer, *Yugoslavia at the Paris Peace Conference: a study in frontiermaking* (New Haven, CT, 1963).

Reparations

The public debate on this topic was sparked by J.M. Keynes, *The Economic Consequences of the Peace* (London, 1971). A strong argument that reparation demands were not a function of France's Rhenish policy is made by Marc Trachtenberg, *Reparation in World Politics: France and European Economic Diplomacy, 1916–1923* (New York, 1980); David Felix, 'Reparations Reconsidered with a Vengeance', *Central European History* 4 (1971): 171–9.

Arms limitations and disarmament

L. Jaffe, *The Decision to Disarm Germany: British Policy towards Post-war German Disarmament, 1914–1919* (London, 1985).

War guilt

J. Willis, *Prologue to Nuremberg: the politics and diplomacy of punishing war criminals of the First World War* (Westport, CT, 1982); A. Lentin, *Lloyd George, Woodrow Wilson and the Guilt of Germany* (Leicester, 1984); N. Ashton and D. Hellema, 'Hanging the Kaiser: Anglo-Dutch Relations and the Fate of Wilhelm II', *Diplomacy & Statecraft* 11 (2000): 53–78.

Reaction in Germany

K. Schwabe, *Woodrow Wilson, Revolutionary Germany, and Peacemaking, 1918–1919* (Chapel Hill, NC, 1985). On the destruction of the German fleet see D. van der Vat, *The Grand Scuttle: The Sinking of the German Fleet at Scapa Flow in 1919* (Annapolis, MD, 1986).

On the realities of the workings of an international conference see S. Marks, 'Behind the Scenes at the Paris Peace Conference of 1919', *Journal of British Studies*

9 (1970): 154–80; on its more general impact C. Lovin, *A School for Diplomats: The Paris Peace Conference of 1919* (Lanham, 1997).

THE NEW EUROPE

A useful background is provided by H. and C. Seton-Watson, *The Making of a New Europe* (London, 1981); an overview of the history of much of the region is found in J. Rothschild, *East Central Europe between the Two World Wars* (Seattle, WA, 1990).

On Poland

A. Walicki, 'The Troubling Legacy of Roman Dmowski', *East European Politics and Societies* 14:1 (2000): 12–46; P. Gadja, *Postscript to Victory: British Policy and the German-Polish Borderlands, 1919–1925* (Washington, DC, 1982). P. Wandycz, *France and her Eastern European Allies, 1919–1925* (Minneapolis, MN, 1962).

On the minorities protection treaties see P. Lauren, 'Human Rights in History: Diplomacy and Racial Equality at the Paris Peace Conference', *Diplomatic History* 2 (1978): 257–78; A. Sharp, 'Britain and the Protection of Minorities at the Paris Peace Conference, 1919', in A.C. Hepburn, ed., *Minorities in History* (London, 1978); C. Fink, 'The Minorities Question at the Paris Peace Conference: The Polish Minority Treaty, June 28, 1919', in M. Boemke *et al.*, *The Treaty of Versailles: a reassessment after 75 years* (Cambridge, 1998), M. Levene, 'Nationalism and Its Alternatives in the International Arena: The Jewish Question at Paris, 1919', *Journal of Contemporary History* 28 (1993): 511–31.

LEAGUE OF NATIONS

General

The League of Nations in Retrospect (New York, 1983); F.P. Walter, *A History of the League of Nations* (London, 1952); A. Zimmern, *The League of Nations and the Rule of Law, 1918–1935* (London, 1936).

Origins

The long historical process which culminated in a League of Nations is discussed in F.H. Hinsley, *Power and the Pursuit of Peace: theory and practice in the history of relations between states* (Cambridge: Cambridge University Press, 1963); see in particular chap. 14, 'The failure of the League of Nations'. The official thinking on the League can be found in Jan Smuts, *The League of Nations: A Practical Suggestion* (London, 1918); G. Egerton, *Great Britain and the Creation of the League of Nations: Strategy, Politics, and International Organization, 1914–1919* (London, 1979). The pressure groups which promoted the idea are dealt with by R.J. Bartlett, *The League to Enforce Peace* (Chapel Hill, NC, 1944) and D.S. Birn, *The League of Nations Union, 1918–1945* (Oxford, 1981).

The problem of article 10 is discussed in J.W.S. Nordholt, *Woodrow Wilson: a life for world peace* (Berkeley, CA: University of California Press, 1990), chap. 29, 'Article X'; D. Mervin, 'Henry Cabot Lodge and the League of Nations', *Journal of American History* 4 (1970).

Organizations connected with the League

M.O. Hudson, *The Permanent Court of International Justice, 1920–1942* (New York, 1943); L. Lloyd, *Peace Through Law: Britain and the International Court in the 1920s* (London: The Royal Historical Society, 1997); G.A. Johnston, *The International Labour Organisation: its work for social and economic progress* (London, 1970); D.A. Morse, *The Origin and Evolution of the I.L.O. and Its Role in the World Community* (Ithaca, NY, 1969).

Mandates

A. Crozier, 'The Establishment of the Mandates System, 1919–25', *Journal of Contemporary History* 14 (1979): 483–513.

Early years

J. Barros, *Office Without Power: Secretary-General Sir Eric Drummond, 1919–1933* (Oxford, 1979); J. Barros, *The Åland Islands Question: Its Settlement by the League of Nations* (New Haven, CT: Yale University Press, 1968).

SOVIET RUSSIA

The intervention

J. Bradley, *Allied Intervention in Russia* (London, 1968); M. Kettle, *Churchill and the Archangel Fiasco, November 1918–July 1918* (London, 1992).

Russo-Polish War

N. Davies, *White Eagle, Red Star: The Polish-Soviet War, 1919–20* (London, 1972).

Anglo-Russian relations

S. White, *Britain and the Bolshevik Revolution* (London: Macmillan, 1979); M. Glenny, 'The Anglo-Soviet Trade Agreement, March 1921', *Journal of Contemporary History* 5:2 (1970): 63–82.

Genoa and Rapallo

Stephen White, *Origins of Detente: The Genoa Conference and Soviet Western Relations, 1921–22* (Cambridge, 1985); Andrew Williams, 'The Genoa Conference of 1922: Lloyd George and the Politics of Recognition', in C. Fink *et al.*, eds, *Genoa, Rapallo and European Reconstruction in 1922* (Cambridge, 1991).

The Comintern

T. Rees and A. Thorpe, *International Communism and the Communist International, 1919–43* (Manchester, 1998).

EASTERN MEDITERRANEAN

General History

D. Fromkin, *A Peace to End All Peace: creating the modern Middle East, 1914–1922* (London, 1989).

Turkey and Greece

P. Helmreich, *From Paris to Sèvres: The Partition of the Ottoman Empire at the Peace Conference of 1919–20* (Columbus, OH, 1974); R. Davison, 'Turkish Diplomacy from Mudros to Lausanne', in G. Craig, ed., *The Diplomats 1919–1939* (New York, 1974); E. Goldstein, 'Great Britain and Greater Greece, 1917–20', *Historical Journal* 32:3 (1989): 339–56; A. Montgomery, 'The Making of the Treaty of Sèvres of 10 August 1920', *Historical Journal* 15:4 (1972): 775–87. On the Greek-Turkish War see: M. Llewellyn Smith, *Ionian Vision: Greece in Asia Minor, 1919–1922* (London, 1973).

On Atatürk the classic biography has been P. Kinross, *Atatürk: A Biography of Mustapha Kemal, Father of Modern Turkey* (London, 1965), now supplemented by the authoritative A. Mango, *Atatürk: The Biography of the Founder of Modern Turkey* (London, 2000).

The McMahon-Hussein correspondence see C. Dawn, 'The Amir of Mecca al-Husayn ibn-'Ali and the Origins of the Arab Revolt', *Proceedings of the American Philosophical Society* 104 (1960) and E. Kedourie, *In the Anglo-Arab Labyrinth: The McMahon-Husayn Correspondence and its Interpretations* (Cambridge, 1976); I. Friedman, 'The McMahon-Hussein Correspondence', *Journal of Contemporary History* 5 (1970): 83–122.

Balfour Declaration and the Palestine mandate

R. Sanders, *The High Walls of Jerusalem: a history of the Balfour Declaration and the birth of the British mandate for Palestine* (New York, 1983).

NAVAL RIVALRY AND EAST ASIAN STABILITY

On the rise of Japan

C. Burdick, *The Japanese Siege of Tsingtau* (Hamden, CT, 1976). On the end of the Anglo-Japanese alliance see I. Nish, *Alliance in Decline* (London, 1972).

For an account of the Washington Conference see: E. Goldstein and J. Maurer, eds, *The Washington Conference, 1921–22: Naval Rivalry, East Asian Stability, and the Road to Pearl Harbor* (London, 1993). On the failures of the Washington system see C. Barnett, *The Collapse of British Power* (London, 1972), especially chap. 5. On Japan see R. Dingman, *Power in the Pacific* (Chicago, IL, 1976); and on the impact of the Washington system on Japan see A. Iriye, *After Imperialism* (Cambridge, MA, 1965). On the Washington Conference as a case study in arms control see H. Bull, 'Strategic Arms Limitation: The Precedent of the Washington and London Naval Treaties', reprinted in R. O'Neill and D. Schwartz, eds, *Hedley Bull on Arms Control* (New York, 1987): 131–51.

LOCARNO

Reparations and war debts

B. Kent, *The Spoils of War: The Politics, Economics and Diplomacy of Reparations, 1918–1932* (Oxford, 1989); D. Aldcroft, *From Versailles to Wall Street, 1918–1929* (Berkeley, CA, 1977); D. Felix, 'Reparations Reconsidered with a Vengeance', *Central European History* 4 (1971); S. Marks, 'Reparations Reconsidered: A Reminder', *Central European History* 2 (1969); S. Schuker, *The End of French Predominance in Europe: the financial crisis of 1924 and the adoption of the Dawes Plan* (Chapel Hill, NC, 1976); D. Silverman, *Reconstructing Europe after the Great War* (Cambridge, MA, 1982); M. Trachtenberg, *Reparation in World Politics: France and European Diplomacy, 1916–1923* (New York, 1980); P. Abrahams, 'American Bankers and the Economic Tactics of Peace, 1919', *Journal of American History* 56 (1969): 572–83.

Ruhr crisis

A. Sharp, 'Lord Curzon and British Policy Towards the Franco-Belgian Occupation of the Ruhr', *Diplomacy & Statecraft* 8 (1997): 83–96.

Disarmament

G. Crosby, *Disarmament and Peace in British Politics, 1914–1919* (Cambridge, 1957); D. Richardson, *The Evolution of British Disarmament Policy in the 1920s* (London, 1989).

Locarno

J. Jacobson, *Locarno Diplomacy: Germany and the West, 1925–1929* (Princeton, NJ, 1972); E. Goldstein, 'British Diplomatic Strategy and the Locarno Conference', in M. Dockrill and B.J.C. McKercher, eds, *Diplomacy and World Power: Studies in British Foreign Policy, 1890–1951* (Cambridge, 1996): 115–35; J. Wright, 'Stresemann and Locarno', *Contemporary European History* 42 (1995): 109–31.

GLOSSARY

Allied and Associated Powers The term 'Allied' was used to designate the grouping during the First World War led by Great Britain, France, and Italy. After the United States entered the war the word 'associated' was added.

Alsace-Lorraine Area of eastern France lost to Germany in 1871 at the end of the Franco-Prussian war.

Armistice An agreement between belligerents for a halt to hostilities.

Capitulations A series of agreements by which the Ottoman Empire had ceded to many foreign powers extra-territorial jurisdiction over their citizens who were resident within the Ottoman Empire. This removed them from the legal jurisdiction of the Ottoman authorities.

Central Powers Term used to designate the grouping of Germany, Austria-Hungary, Bulgaria, and the Ottoman Empire during the First World War.

Comintern Also know as the Third International, this organization was established in Moscow in March 1919 to promote communist revolutions. It was dissolved in 1943.

Condominium The joint administration of a territory by more than one country.

Council of Ambassadors The body of the key Allied Powers, represented by their ambassadors at Paris, which after the ending of the Paris Peace Conference met to discuss ongoing issues related to the peace settlement. It finally ceased after the Locarno Pact.

Council of Four To expedite negotiations at the 1919 Paris Peace Conference the chief Allied leaders began to meet on 24 March. Membership comprised the leaders of France (Clemenceau), Great Britain (Lloyd George), the United States (Wilson), and Italy (Orlando), though the latter was absent for most of the sessions.

Council of Five At the 1919 Paris Peace Conference, the body in which the foreign ministers of France, Great Britain, Italy, Japan, and the United States met.

Council of Ten Initially the main decision-making body at the 1919 Paris Peace Conference, comprising the leaders and foreign ministers of France, Great Britain, Italy, Japan, and the United States. It was effectively superseded at the end of March by the Council of Four and the Council of Five.

de facto The implied recognition of a government as enjoying effective control over a country and thereby being, in fact, the responsible authority.

de jure The acceptance of a government's claim to exercise authority over its territory. The usual precursor to the establishment of diplomatic relations.

Little Entente Originally a term of derision coined by a Hungarian journalist, it came to be used to describe the system of alliances linking Czechoslovakia, Roumania, and Yugoslavia.

Mandate Territories under the 1919–20 peace treaties, formerly belonging to the German or Ottoman Empires, placed in the care of the League of Nations and assigned to the administration of Britain, Australia, New Zealand, South Africa, and France.

Monroe Doctrine An American foreign policy tradition, first enunciated by President Monroe in 1823, declaring both European non-interference in the western hemisphere and United States non-interference in the old world.

Open Door Term, first used by United States Secretary of State John Hay, to describe policy toward China. Aim was to ensure that all states received equal treatment in their dealings with China.

Plenary A session attended by all members.

Polish Corridor Term used to describe the narrow parcel of land providing Poland with a coast, and thus separating the bulk of Germany from East Prussia.

Riparian States which share access to a common river are known as the riparian states of that river.

INDEX

SEMINAR STUDIES   IN HISTORY

General Editors: Clive Emsley & Gordon Martel

The series was founded by Patrick Richardson in 1966. Between 1980 and 1996 Roger Lockyer edited the series before handing over to Clive Emsley (Professor of History at the Open University) and Gordon Martel (Professor of International History at the University of Northern British Columbia, Canada and Senior Research Fellow at De Montfort University).

MEDIEVAL ENGLAND

TUDOR ENGLAND

STUART BRITAIN

Social Change and Continuity: England 1550–1750 (Second edition)
Barry Coward   0 582 29442 8

James I (Second edition)
S J Houston   0 582 20911 0

The English Civil War 1640–1649
Martyn Bennett   0 582 35392 0

Charles I, 1625–1640
Brian Quintrell   0 582 00354 7

The English Republic 1649–1660 (Second edition)
Toby Barnard   0 582 08003 7

Radical Puritans in England 1550–1660
R J Acheson   0 582 35515 X

The Restoration and the England of Charles II (Second edition)
John Miller   0 582 29223 9

The Glorious Revolution (Second edition)
John Miller   0 582 29222 0

EARLY MODERN EUROPE

The Renaissance (Second edition)
Alison Brown   0 582 30781 3

The Emperor Charles V
Martyn Rady   0 582 35475 7

French Renaissance Monarchy: Francis I and Henry II (Second edition)
Robert Knecht   0 582 28707 3

The Protestant Reformation in Europe
Andrew Johnston   0 582 07020 1

The French Wars of Religion 1559–1598 (Second edition)
Robert Knecht   0 582 28533 X

Phillip II
Geoffrey Woodward   0 582 07232 8

The Thirty Years' War
Peter Limm   0 582 35373 4

Louis XIV
Peter Campbell   0 582 01770 X

Spain in the Seventeenth Century
Graham Darby   0 582 07234 4

Peter the Great
William Marshall   0 582 00355 5

EUROPE 1789–1918

Britain and the French Revolution
Clive Emsley   0 582 36961 4

Revolution and Terror in France 1789–1795 (Second edition)
D G Wright   0 582 00379 2

Napoleon and Europe
D G Wright   0 582 35457 9

The Abolition of Serfdom in Russia, 1762–1907
David Moon   0 582 29486 X

Nineteenth-Century Russia: Opposition to Autocracy
Derek Offord   0 582 35767 5

The Constitutional Monarchy in France 1814–48
Pamela Pilbeam   0 582 31210 8

The 1848 Revolutions (Second edition)
Peter Jones   0 582 06106 7

The Italian Risorgimento
M Clark   0 582 00353 9

Bismarck & Germany 1862–1890 (Second edition)
D G Williamson   0 582 29321 9

Imperial Germany 1890–1918
Ian Porter, Ian Armour and Roger Lockyer   0 582 03496 5

The Dissolution of the Austro-Hungarian Empire 1867–1918 (Second edition)
John W Mason   0 582 29466 5

Second Empire and Commune: France 1848–1871 (Second edition)
William H C Smith   0 582 28705 7

France 1870–1914 (Second edition)
Robert Gildea   0 582 29221 2

The Scramble for Africa (Second edition)
M E Chamberlain   0 582 36881 2

Late Imperial Russia 1890–1917
John F Hutchinson   0 582 32721 0

The First World War
Stuart Robson   0 582 31556 5

Austria, Prussia and Germany, 1806–1871
John Breuilly   0 582 43739 3

EUROPE SINCE 1918

The Russian Revolution (Second edition)
Anthony Wood   0 582 35559 1

Lenin's Revolution: Russia, 1917–1921
David Marples   0 582 31917 X

Stalin and Stalinism (Second edition) *Martin McCauley*	0 582 27658 6
The Weimar Republic (Second edition) *John Hiden*	0 582 28706 5
The Inter-War Crisis 1919–1939 *Richard Overy*	0 582 35379 3
Fascism and the Right in Europe, 1919–1945 *Martin Blinkhorn*	0 582 07021 X
Spain's Civil War (Second edition) *Harry Browne*	0 582 28988 2
The Third Reich (Third edition) *D G Williamson*	0 582 20914 5
The Origins of the Second World War (Second edition) *R J Overy*	0 582 29085 6
The Second World War in Europe *Paul MacKenzie*	0 582 32692 3
The French at War, 1934–1944 *Nicholas Atkin*	0 582 36899 5
Anti-Semitism before the Holocaust *Albert S Lindemann*	0 582 36964 9
The Holocaust: The Third Reich and the Jews *David Engel*	0 582 32720 2
Germany from Defeat to Partition, 1945–1963 *D G Williamson*	0 582 29218 2
Britain and Europe since 1945 *Alex May*	0 582 30778 3
Eastern Europe 1945–1969: From Stalinism to Stagnation *Ben Fowkes*	0 582 32693 1
Eastern Europe since 1970 *Bülent Gökay*	0 582 32858 6
The Khrushchev Era, 1953–1964 *Martin McCauley*	0 582 27776 0

NINETEENTH-CENTURY BRITAIN

Britain before the Reform Acts: Politics and Society 1815–1832 *Eric J Evans*	0 582 00265 6
Parliamentary Reform in Britain c. 1770–1918 *Eric J Evans*	0 582 29467 3
Democracy and Reform 1815–1885 *D G Wright*	0 582 31400 3

Poverty and Poor Law Reform in Nineteenth-Century Britain, 1834–1914:
From Chadwick to Booth
David Englander   0 582 31554 9

The Birth of Industrial Britain: Economic Change, 1750–1850
Kenneth Morgan   0 582 29833 4

Chartism (Third edition)
Edward Royle   0 582 29080 5

Peel and the Conservative Party 1830–1850
Paul Adelman   0 582 35557 5

Gladstone, Disraeli and later Victorian Politics (Third edition)
Paul Adelman   0 582 29322 7

Britain and Ireland: From Home Rule to Independence
Jeremy Smith   0 582 30193 9

TWENTIETH-CENTURY BRITAIN

The Rise of the Labour Party 1880–1945 (Third edition)
Paul Adelman   0 582 29210 7

The Conservative Party and British Politics 1902–1951
Stuart Ball   0 582 08002 9

The Decline of the Liberal Party 1910–1931 (Second edition)
Paul Adelman   0 582 27733 7

The British Women's Suffrage Campaign 1866–1928
Harold L Smith   0 582 29811 3

War & Society in Britain 1899–1948
Rex Pope   0 582 03531 7

The British Economy since 1914: A Study in Decline?
Rex Pope   0 582 30194 7

Unemployment in Britain between the Wars
Stephen Constantine   0 582 35232 0

The Attlee Governments 1945–1951
Kevin Jefferys   0 582 06105 9

The Conservative Governments 1951–1964
Andrew Boxer   0 582 20913 7

Britain under Thatcher
Anthony Seldon and Daniel Collings   0 582 31714 2

Britain and Empire, 1880–1945
Dane Kennedy   0 582 41493 8

INTERNATIONAL HISTORY

The Eastern Question 1774–1923 (Second edition)
A L Macfie   0 582 29195 X

India 1885–1947: The Unmaking of an Empire
Ian Copland   0 582 38173 8

The Origins of the First World War (Second edition)
Gordon Martel   0 582 28697 2

The United States and the First World War
Jennifer D Keene   0 582 35620 2

Anti-Semitism before the Holocaust
Albert S Lindemann   0 582 36964 9

The Origins of the Cold War, 1941–1949 (Second edition)
Martin McCauley   0 582 27659 4

Russia, America and the Cold War, 1949–1991
Martin McCauley   0 582 27936 4

The Arab–Israeli Conflict
Kirsten E Schulze   0 582 31646 4

The United Nations since 1945: Peacekeeping and the Cold War
Norrie MacQueen   0 582 35673 3

Decolonisation: The British Experience since 1945
Nicholas J White   0 582 29087 2

The Origins of the Vietnam War
Fredrik Logevall   0 582 31918 8

The Vietnam War
Mitchell Hall   0 582 32859 4

WORLD HISTORY

China in Transformation 1900–1949
Colin Mackerras   0 582 31209 4

Japan Faces the World, 1925–1952
Mary L Hanneman   0 582 36898 7

Japan in Transformation, 1952–2000
Jeff Kingston   0 582 41875 5

China since 1949
Linda Benson   0 582 35722 5

US HISTORY

American Abolitionists
Stanley Harrold   0 582 35738 1

The American Civil War, 1861–1865
Reid Mitchell   0 582 31973 0

America in the Progressive Era, 1890–1914
Lewis L Gould   0 582 35671 7

The United States and the First World War
Jennifer D Keene   0 582 35620 2

The Truman Years, 1945–1953
Mark S Byrnes   0 582 32904 3

The Korean War
Steven Hugh Lee   0 582 31988 9

The Origins of the Vietnam War
Fredrik Logevall   0 582 31918 8

The Vietnam War
Mitchell Hall   0 582 32859 4